FUNDAMENTALISM
THE SEARCH FOR MEANING

Malise Ruthven

OXFORD
UNIVERSITY PRESS

OXFORD
UNIVERSITY PRESS

Great Clarendon Street, Oxford OX2 6DP

Oxford University Press is a department of the University of Oxford.
It furthers the University's objective of excellence in research, scholarship,
and education by publishing worldwide in

Oxford New York

Auckland Bangkok Buenos Aires Cape Town Chennai
Dar es Salaam Delhi Hong Kong Istanbul Karachi Kolkata
Kuala Lumpur Madrid Melbourne Mexico City Mumbai Nairobi
São Paulo Shanghai Taipei Tokyo Toronto

Oxford is a registered trade mark of Oxford University Press
in the UK and in certain other countries

Published in the United States
by Oxford University Press Inc., New York

British Library Cataloguing in Publication Data

Data available

Library of Congress Cataloguing in Publication Data

Data available

ISBN 0-19-284091-6

Typeset in Scala by
Footnote Graphics Limited, Warminster, Wilts
Printed in Great Britain by
Clays Ltd., St Ives plc

PREFACE

This essay is the fruit of several years' reflection about the religious revivals that seem to be occurring in all the major religious traditions and the capacity these revivals have for generating highly charged social and political conflicts in a shrinking 'globalized' world where people of differing and competing faiths are having to live in close proximity with each other. While recognizing that 'fundamentalism' is a fact of life in the twenty-first century—one that was illustrated in the most spectacular way on 11 September 2001—it seeks to untangle some of the meanings associated with the term, despite its obvious drawbacks. 'Fundamentalism' originated in the very specific theological context of early twentieth-century Protestant America, and its applicability beyond its original matrix is—to put it mildly—problematic. Nevertheless, as I hope to show through numerous examples and parallels, there are compelling 'family resemblances' between militancies or fundamentalisms in different religious traditions. They may not add up to a coherent ideological alternative to the triumph of liberal democracy as described by Francis Fukuyama in his celebrated 1992 essay *The End of History and the Last Man*. But they are symptomatic, I believe, of the spiritual dystopias and dysfunctional cultural relationships that characterize the world of what some contemporary commentators are choosing to call 'Late Capitalism'.

Many people, students, friends, and colleagues, contributed to this book during its gestation. Students at Dartmouth College, Aberdeen University, the University of California, San Diego, and at the Colorado College helped to focus my thinking with their questions and essays. Academic friends and colleagues, including the late Jim Thrower, the late Albert Hourani, Hans Penner, Gene Garthwaite, Philip Khoury, Arthur Droge, Robert Lee, Charles Tripp, Sami Zubaida, Max Taylor, David Weddle, Ketil Volden, Efraim Inbar, and Fred Halliday, helped stimulate my thinking by inviting me to conferences, lectures, and seminars. I would like to express my thanks to them all and to Martin Marty and Scott Appleby for inviting me to two meetings of the Fundamentalism Project in Chicago in 1990 and 1993 which first aroused my interest in the subject and gave me the opportunity to meet and talk with scholars from several disciplines and countries.

Elfi Pallis kindly supplied some of the information on Jewish fundamentalism that appears in Chapter 6.

CONTENTS

1

Family Resemblances

'Heave an egg out of a Pullman window', wrote H. L. Mencken, the famous American journalist, in the 1920s, 'and you will hit a Fundamentalist almost anywhere in the United States today.' Fundamentalism is a word with which everyone is familiar now. Hardly a day passes without news of some terrorist atrocity committed by 'religious fanatics' or 'fundamentalists' in some part of the world. As I write this paragraph in the serene and pleasant surroundings of the British Library in London, the newspapers are full of the latest example of religiously motivated murder, with pictures of mutilated and blood-spattered people after the bombing of a disco-club on the island of Bali, which killed nearly 200 people, most of them young Australians.

The most spectacular 'fundamentalist' atrocity of all was the suicide hijacking of three airliners by Islamist militants belonging to the al-Qaeda network led by the Saudi dissident Osama bin Laden, on 11 September 2001. More than 3,000 people were killed when the planes crashed into the World Trade Center in New York and the Pentagon near Washington. But there have been dozens of other atrocities blamed on fundamentalists which have caught the headlines: the killing of more than fifty tourists at Luxor in Egypt in November 1997; the hundred or more suicide bombings in Israel during the Palestinian uprising, or *intifada*, beginning September 2000 that have killed some 430 people, about half of all Israeli victims of the Palestinian *intifada*; the suicide truck-bomb that killed more than 300 US and French marines in Beirut in 1983, causing the international peace-keeping force to leave; the attacks on the US embassies in Kenya and Tanzania in 1998 that left several hundred dead, most of them innocent Africans.

Most of these atrocities have been blamed on Islamic terrorists whose hostility to the West, and to the United States in particular, is widely presumed to be the outcome of their fundamentalist views. Though far from being exclusive to Islam—Jewish and Sikh religious extremists have been responsible for assassinating the Prime Ministers of Israel and India, respectively, while Sikh and Hindu extremists have also been held responsible for violence on a much larger scale in India and Sri Lanka—the world of Islam seems particularly prone to religiously inspired violence at this time.

Foremost among the conflicts attributable to fundamentalist intransigence is the Arab–Israel dispute, still the world's most dangerous flashpoint. For the rationally minded person, whatever their religious beliefs, the Middle East impasse illustrates the pitfalls into which funda-mentalist politics is driving the world. A secular discourse that recognizes the competing claims of group self-interest should be able to balance them equitably, at least in theory. Where conflicts are rooted in competing religious identities, as in Israel-Palestine and Northern Ireland, peace processes, to have any chance of success, must be conducted in secular terms. For the outsider (whether atheist, agnostic, or liberal religionist), a rational solution to the Palestinian conflict based on 'trading territory for peace' must seem to be within the bounds of possibility if only the religious fanatics or fundamentalists were kept out of the frame. Indeed, such is the reasoning behind the so-called 'road map' towards a two-state solution being promoted, at the time of writing, by the US government, with support from the United Nations, Russia, and the European Union. It is the religious factor, not the conflict of interests, that threatens to prevent a settlement. On the Jewish side, orthodox settlers from Gush Emunim, the Bloc of the Faithful, absolutely refuse to abandon the West Bank settlements that are obstructing the peace process because, they insist, the land was originally given to the Children of Israel by God. They are duty bound to hold it in trust until the coming of the Messiah, whose return is imminent. On the Arab side, religious Palestinian Muslims

ideologies of Marxist-Leninism, National Socialism, and anti-colonialism as the principal challenge to a world order based on the hegemonic power of the liberal capitalist West. Just as the contradictions within liberalism (between, for example, the universal rights of man and the pursuit of imperial trade) gave rise to the anti-colonial movements of the post-Second World War era, so the earliest shoots of fundamentalism (semantically, if not as an age-old phenomenon) came to fruition in the United States—in the very heart of the capitalist West.

Academics are still debating the appropriateness of using the 'F-word' in contexts outside its original Protestant setting. Islamic scholars argue that since all observant Muslims believe the Koran—the divine text of Islam—to be the unmediated Word of God, all are committed to a doctrine of scriptural inerrancy, whereas for Protestants biblical inerrancy is one of the hallmarks that distinguishes fundamentalists from liberals. If all believing Muslims are 'fundamentalists' in this sense of the word, then the term is meaningless, because it fails to distinguish between the hard-edged militant who seeks to 'Islamize' his society and the quietist who avoids politics completely. 'Higher criticism of the Bible' based on close textual study—the original cause of the Protestant fundamentalist revolt against liberalism and modernism—challenged traditional teachings by claiming, for example, that the Book of Isaiah has more than one author and that the Pentateuch—the first five books of the Old

Testament—was not authored by Moses himself. 'Higher criticism' of the Koran, by contrast, which would challenge the belief that every word contained in the text was dictated to Muhammad by God through the agency of the Angel Gabriel, has not been a major issue in the Muslim world to date, though it may become so in due course, as literary-critical theories gain ground in academic circles. The present concerns of most Muslim 'fundamentalists' are largely of a different order: the removal of governments deemed corrupt or too pro-Western and the replacement of laws imported from the West by the indigenous Sharia code derived from the Koran and the *sunna* (custom) of the Prophet Muhammad.

Parallel concerns may be found among the 'fundamentalist' New Religious Movements (NRMs) in Japan, where the Allied Occupation in 1945 imposed comprehensive and far-reaching changes in the country's civil code. On slightly different grounds scholars of Judaism point out that 'fundamentalist' is much too broad a term when applied both to ultra-orthodox groups known as Haredim (some of which still refuse to recognize the legitimacy of the State of Israel) and the religious settlers of Gush Emunim (the Bloc of the Faithful) who place more emphasis on holding onto the Land of Israel than on observing the Halakha (Jewish law).

'Fundamentalism', according to its critics, is just a dirty fourteen-letter word. It is a term of abuse levelled by liberals and Enlightenment rationalists against any group,

BOX 1

The word *fundamentalism* [emphasis original] has come to imply an orientation to the world that is anti-intellectual, bigoted, and intolerant. It is applied to those whose life-style and politics are unacceptable to modern, Western eyes and, most particularly, to those who would break down the barrier we have erected [in America] between church and state. The term fundamentalism is reserved for those who have the temerity to attempt to project their world-view onto others. Against such people we lash out with a label that immediately delegitimates them, that immediately says these people are out of the mainstream and therefore deserve to be given *ad hominem* dismissal. 'We' immediately know that 'they' are not like us, or even worthy of our time, since clearly 'we' cannot deal with 'them'. Further 'we' would like very much to believe that we would never behave as they do and that we have never done so.

(Jay M. Harris, 'Fundamentalism: Objections from a Modern Jewish Historian', in J. S. Hawley (ed.), *Fundamentalism and Gender*)

religious or otherwise, which dares to challenge the 'absolutism' of the post-Enlightenment outlook. Other scholars argue that fundamentalism is a caricature or mirror-image of the same post-Enlightenment outlook it professes to oppose: by adopting the same rational style of argument used by the secular 'enemy', fundamentalists repress or bleach out the multifaceted, polysemic ways in which myth and religions appeal to all aspects of the human psyche,

not just to the rational mind, with fundamentalists exposing what one anthropologist calls 'the hubris of reason's
pretence in trying to take over religion's role'.[1]

Words have a life and energy of their own that will
usually defy the exacting demands of scholars. The F-word
has long since escaped from the Protestant closet in which
it began its semantic career around the turn of the
twentieth century.

The applications or meanings attached to words cannot be confined to the context in which they originate: if
one limits 'fundamentalism' to its original meaning one
might as well do the same for words like 'nationalism'
and 'secularization' which also appeared in the post-
Enlightenment West before being applied to movements
or processes in non-Western societies. Applying the same
restrictive logic, one should not speak of Judaism or
Christianity as 'religions' because that originally Latin
word is found in neither Old nor New Testaments. 'Fundamentalism' may indeed be a 'Western linguistic encroach-
ment' on other traditions, but the phenomenon (or rather,
the phenomena) it describes exists, although no single
definition will ever be uncontested. Put at its broadest, it
may be described as a 'religious way of being' that mani-
fests itself in a strategy by which beleaguered believers
attempt to preserve their distinctive identity as a people or
group in the face of modernity and secularization.

Bruce Lawrence, a scholar who believes that the F-word
can be extended beyond its original Protestant matrix,

sees its connection with modernity as crucial: 'Fundamentalism is a multifocal phenomenon precisely *because*
the modernist hegemony, though originating in some
parts of the West, was not limited to Protestant Christianity' (emphasis added). The Enlightenment influenced
significant numbers of Jews, and because of the coloniza-
tion of much of Africa and Asia in the nineteenth and early
twentieth centuries, it touched the lives and destinies of
many Muslims.[2] According to this view the 'modernist
hegemony' did not end with the attainment of political
independence by so-called Third World countries. Indeed,
given the far-reaching consequences of the scientific revolution that flowed from the Enlightenment, the modern
predicament against which fundamentalists everywhere
are reacting has been extended to cover virtually every
corner of the planet.

Rather than quibbling about the usefulness of 'fundamentalism' as an analytic term, I propose in this book
to explore its ambiguities, to unpack some of its meanings. The term may be less than wholly satisfactory, but
the phenomena it encompasses deserve to be analysed.
Whether or not we like the phrase, fundamentalist or
fundamentalist-like movements appear to be erupting in
many parts of the world, from the Americas to South-East
Asia. No one would claim that these movements, which
occur in most of the world's great religious traditions, are
identical. But all of them exhibit what the philosopher
Ludwig Wittgenstein called 'family resemblances'. In

explaining his analogy Wittgenstein took the example of games—board-games, card-games, ball-games, Olympic Games, and so forth. Instead of assuming that all must have a single, defining feature because of the common name applied to them, games should be examined for similarities and relationships. Such an examination, said Wittgenstein, would reveal 'a complicated network of similarities overlapping and criss-crossing: sometimes overall similarities, sometimes similarities of detail' such as one finds in different members of the same family, in which 'build, features, colour of eyes, gait, temperament et cetera overlap and criss-cross in the same way'.[3]

Before proceeding to explore these resemblances, it would be useful to recapitulate the history of the word and its burgeoning semantic career. Its origins are quite revealing. Although the word has acquired negative connotations in much of the world, it did not begin as a term of abuse or even criticism. It appeared early in the twentieth century—not, as might be expected, in the 'Bible Belt' of the Old South, but in southern California, one of America's most rapidly developing regions (in the same area and at about the same time that one of fundamentalism's principal bugbears, the Hollywood film industry, made its appearance). In 1910 Milton and Lyman Stewart, two devout Christian brothers who had made their fortune in the California oil business, embarked on a five-year programme of sponsorship for a series of pamphlets which were sent free of charge to 'English-speaking Protestant pastors, evangelists, missionaries, theological professors, theological students, YMCA secretaries, Sunday School superintendents, religious lay workers, and editors of religious publications throughout the world'. Entitled *The Fundamentals: A Testimony of Truth*, the tracts, written by a number of leading conservative American and British theologians, were aimed at stopping the erosion of what the brothers and their editors considered to be the 'fundamental' beliefs of Protestantism: the inerrancy of the Bible; the direct creation of the world, and humanity, *ex nihilo* by God (in contrast to Darwinian evolution); the authenticity of miracles; the virgin birth of Jesus, his Crucifixion and bodily resurrection; the substitutionary atonement (the doctrine that Christ died to redeem the sins of humanity); and (for some but not all believers) his imminent return to judge and rule over the world.

Like many conservative American Protestants, who are technically known as premillennial dispensationalists, the Stewart brothers believed that the End Times prophesies contained in the scriptures, notably the Old Testament books of Ezekiel and Daniel, and the last book of the New Testament, the Revelation of St John, referred to real (not symbolic) events that were shortly due to happen on the plane of human history. Drawing on a tradition of prophecy interpretation developed by an English clergyman, John Nelson Darby (1800–82), they argued that since many Old Testament prophecies about the coming Messiah were fulfilled with the coming of Christ as documented in the New Testament, other predictions, concerning the End Times, would soon come to pass. Expecting the world to end at any moment they saw it as their duty to save as many people as possible before the coming catastrophe when sinners would perish horribly and the saved would be 'raptured' into the presence of Christ.

Being successful businessmen, the Stewarts wanted, and expected, results. As Lyman wrote to Milton after learning that the American Tobacco Company was spending millions of dollars distributing free cigarettes in order to give people a taste for them: 'Christians should learn from the wisdom of the world.' Theological motives were complemented by business competition. Lyman's 'organizing principle' in the oil business was fighting his rival John D. Rockefeller's attempts to monopolize the industry. It may or may not be coincidental that one of the first preachers he hired came to his attention after preaching against 'something that one of those infidel professors in Chicago University had published'. Chicago Divinity School, a hotbed of liberalism, had been founded and endowed by John D. Rockefeller.

Some three million copies of *The Fundamentals* were circulated, on both sides of the Atlantic. The -*ist* was added in 1920 by Curtis Lee Laws, a conservative Baptist editor: 'Fundamentalists', he declared, 'were those who were ready to do battle royal for The Fundamentals.' The previous year William B. Riley, a leader of the militant dispensationalist premillennialist party among the Northern

Baptists, had organized the non-denominational World Christian Fundamentals Association. Although premillennialist ideas do not loom as large in *The Fundamentals* as they would in later fundamentalist discourse, there is no doubt that the Stewart brothers approved. About half the American contributors to *The Fundamentals*, including such leading lights as Reuben Torrey and Cyrus Ignatius Scofield, were premillennialists. Before endowing *The Fundamentals*, Lyman Stewart had been a major sponsor of Scofield's reference Bible, first published in 1909, and still the preferred commentary of American premillennialists.

The belief that Jesus would return to rule over an earthly kingdom of the righteous after defeating the Antichrist dates back to the earliest phase of Christianity, when the apostles lived in the daily expectation of his promised return. Dismayed by its revolutionary potential, which challenged the renovated imperial cults, common to both Eastern Orthodoxy and Western Catholicism, that conferred divine legitimacy on the Holy Roman and Byzantine emperors, the early church fathers, notably St Augustine (354–430) allegorized and spiritualized the coming Kingdom of God. Christian apocalyptic became 'part of the everyday fabric of Christian life and belief, and to that extent reinforced eschatological awareness by embedding it in liturgy and preaching' while distancing Catholic thought from literalistic readings of prophesy and especially notions of an earthly millennium.[5] The seal on Augustine's teaching was set by the Council of Ephesus

in the past or projected into the future, will be explored in the next chapter. Here it is enough to point out that the 'F-word', however constructed, should never be taken at face value: even at its origin, in *The Fundamentals*, its meaning was contested. In no tradition does one find a complete consensus, even among conservatives, about what the 'fundamentals' of the faith really are. Fundamentalists are nothing if not selective about the texts they use and their mode of interpretation. They are also much more innovative in the way they interpret the texts they select than is often supposed. In this respect they may be contrasted with traditionalists.

'Tradition', like 'fundamental', can also be understood in more than one way. Among Roman Catholics, Anglicans, and other religious communities, the word conveys the sense of a cumulative body of ritual, behaviour, and thought that reaches back to the time of origins. In Catholicism especially, tradition embodying the accumulated experience and knowledge of the Church is seen as a source of authority equal to scripture. Tied to the exclusive authority of the Church, tradition was affirmed at the Council of Trent in the sixteenth century, the Church's official response to the challenge posed by the *sola scriptura* doctrine of the Protestant reformers. In a sense Martin Luther, John Calvin, and other Reformation leaders could be described as 'fundamentalists' many centuries before the term was coined, while the Council of Trent can be seen as a 'fundamentalist' or 'integralist' response.

In the Islamic tradition similar considerations apply: tradition here means the accumulated body of interpretation, law, and practice as developed over the centuries by the *ulama*, the class of 'learned men' who constitute Islam's professional religionists or clerics. Throughout Islamic history there have been 'renovators' or reformers who, like Luther, challenged the authority of the *ulama* on the basis of their readings of the Sources of Islam, namely the Koran and the Hadiths (the latter, sometimes confusingly translated as 'Traditions', are canonized reports about Muhammad's deeds and teachings, based, it is supposed, on the oral testimony of his contemporaries and passed down by word of mouth before being collated into written collections). In this sense the medieval scholar Ibn Taymiyya (d. 1326) who ended his life in prison for challenging the authority of the *ulama* and rulers of his day was a 'fundamentalist'. Significantly his writings are extremely popular among today's Islamist militants.

A less specialized meaning of 'tradition', however, is also relevant here. In a broader context, tradition is simply what occurs unselfconsciously as part of the natural order of things, an unreflective or unconsidered *Weltanschauung* (world view). In the words of Martin Marty, 'most people who live in a traditional culture do not know they are traditionalists'.[5] Tradition, in this sense, consists in not being aware that how one believes or behaves is 'traditional', because alternative ways of thinking or living are simply not taken into consideration. In 'traditional' societies, including the mainly rural communities that formerly constituted the American Bible Belt, the Bible was seen as comprehensively true, a source of universal wisdom, knowledge, and authority deemed to have been transmitted to humanity by God through the prophets, patriarchs, and apostles who wrote the Bible. The latter was not thought of as a 'scientific textbook'; but nor did the ordinary pastor or worshipper consider it 'unscientific'. For most of the eighteenth and nineteenth centuries the Bible was considered compatible with reason, or at least with that version of reason conveyed by the 'common-sense' philosophy which spread to North America from Scotland, along with Calvinist theology and more or less democratic forms of church governance.

When Higher Criticism, originating in Germany, began to challenge the received understandings of the Bible, for example by using sophisticated methods of textual analysis to argue that books attributed to Moses or Isaiah show evidence of editorial changes, textual accumulations, and multiple authorship, or that the doctrine of the virgin birth of Christ depended on a mistranslation of the original Greek text, unreflective tradition (the 'received knowledge' of generations) was converted into reactive defensiveness. From this perspective fundamentalism may be defined as 'tradition made self-aware and consequently defensive'. In Samuel Heilman's words, 'traditionalism is not funda-mentalism, but a necessary correlate to it'.[6]

In all religions, but especially in Protestantism, the

active defence of tradition demands selectivity, since the text of the Bible is too vast and complex to be defended in all its details. Like any military commander, the fundamentalist had to choose the ground on which to do 'battle royal' with the forces of liberalism and Higher Criticism. *The Fundamentals* was part of the process that galvanized this reaction. Hence in America especially it cut across the more democratically organized denominations, including Presbyterians, Baptists, Lutherans, and Methodists. In most of the American denominations it represented the grass roots reaction to the elitism of the seminaries, perceived as being out of touch with the culture and beliefs of ordinary believers. Yet, as Marty and Appleby point out, the very idea behind the project revealed the distance that had already been travelled along the path of secularity: 'Designating fundamentalisms automatically places the designator at great remove from the time when religion thrived as a whole way of life. To identify any one thing or set of beliefs or practices as essential is to diminish other elements of what was once an organic whole.'[7]

The most famous of the 'battles royal' which tore many American churches apart in the first half of the twentieth century was the 'Monkey Trial' in Dayton Tennessee in 1925. As Garry Wills, one of America's best-known commentators has explained, the trial was something of a 'put-up job' engineered, in effect, by the American Civil Liberties Union (ACLU) to challenge an obscure and little-used Tennessee state law banning the teaching of evo-

BOX 2

Opposing Christian Views of Evolution

1. ANTI

All the ills from which America suffers can be traced back to the teaching of evolution. It would be better to destroy every other book ever written and save just the first three verses of Genesis.

(William Jennings Bryan, in Vincent Crapanzano, *Serving the Word: Literalism in America from the Pulpit to the Bench*)

Evolution is the root of atheism, of communism, nazism, anarchism, behaviorism, racism, economic imperialism, militarism, libertinism, anarchism, and all manner of anti-Christian systems of belief and practice.

(Henry Morris, *The Remarkable Birth of Planet Earth*)

2. PRO

Evolutionary theory emphasizes our kinship with nonhuman animals and denies that we were created separately. But it does not interfere with the central Judaeo-Christian message that we are objects of special concern to the Creator. It simply denies us an exclusive right to that title.

(Philip Kitcher, *Abusing Science: The Case against Creationism*)

lution in schools. Many southern states had such laws early in the twentieth century. A biology teacher, John Scopes (who subsequently admitted that he had missed teaching the classes dealing with evolution), 'claimed (rather shakily) to have broken the law'.[8] It was 'one of the best early examples of what would later be known as a "media event"',[9] in which the coverage itself was more important than what actually occurred in court. Hundreds of journalists attended, including the most famous reporter of the day, H. L. Mencken of the *Baltimore Sun*. Radio lines were brought into the courtroom, and the judge held up proceedings to allow photographers to get their shots. The fundamentalist defenders of the state law won the trial on points. With a fundamentalist jury, three members of which testified that they read nothing but the Bible, the verdict was a foregone conclusion. The state law was upheld but Scopes had his conviction quashed on appeal, which prevented the ACLU from pursuing its original aim of bringing the case to a higher Federal court. He went on to become a geologist after winning a scholarship to the University of Chicago.

Culturally the media battle was a devastating defeat for fundamentalism. In a famous cross-examination before the trial judge William Jennings Bryan, former Secretary of State and three times Democratic candidate for the presidency, suffered public humiliation at the hands of Clarence Darrow, the ACLU lawyer. Cleverly drawing on literalistic interpretations of the Bible approved of by conservatives, Darrow showed that Bryan's knowledge of scripture and fundamentalist principles of interpretation was fatally flawed. Afflicted with diabetes, Bryan died shortly after the trial, a broken man. In the media treatment sight was lost of the moral issues that had been his primary concern. As a Democrat and populist Bryan believed that German militarism, the ultimate cause of the First World War, had been a by-product of Darwin's theory of natural selection combined with Friedrich Nietzsche's ideas about the human Will to Power. Given the way in which ideas of Social Darwinism were subsequently put to use by the Nazis, he deserves more credit than he has been given. Shortly before the Second World War, Adolf Hitler would state in one of his speeches: '[Anyone] who has pondered on the order of this world realizes that its meaning lies in the warlike survival of the fittest.'[10] Anti-evolution laws remained on the statue books of several American states, and indeed were extended in some cases. But for the American public at large fundamentalists were exposed as rural ignoramuses, countryside 'hillbillies' out of touch with modern thought. One of the major cultural events of twentieth-century America, the 'Monkey Trial', precipitated what might be called the 'withdrawal phase' of American fundamentalism—a retreat into the enclaves of churches and private educational institutions, such as Bob Jones University. In the mainstream academies, seminaries, and denominations, liberal theology which accepted evolution as 'God's way of doing things' swept the board.

As Susan Harding explains, the regime of public religiosity that prevailed in America during the mid-twentieth century was secular in the limited sense, at least,

BOX 3

'In their theories, story lines, plots, and images, the nation's scholars, journalists, novelists, playwrights, and filmmakers most explicitly articulated modern America as a world in which Fundamentalists figured as stigmatized outsiders. The terms of secular modernity were also written into a wide array of laws, court decisions, government policies, decrees, and regulations, codes of etiquette, customs, practices, and commonsense presuppositions that structured national public discourses.'

(Susan F. Harding, *The Book of Jerry Falwell*)

that 'at the national level signs of religious partisanship were voluntarily suppressed' though it remained for the most part 'incomplete, fragile, and, at times and places, seriously contested'.[11] Thereafter the 'modern secular hegemony' held sway for several decades.

The triumph of liberalism in the mainstream churches was at first tacitly endorsed by the fundamentalists who, for the most part, opted for the strategy of 'separation' from the world. Logically premillennialist Christians should not care if 'the world' goes from bad to worse, though they are charitably enjoined to rescue as many souls as they can. According to the Book of Revelation the reign of the Antichrist preceding the Second Coming will be accompanied by all sorts of portents and signs of evil. As the 'saved remnant' of humanity, true Christians (i.e.

ambitions, American fundamentalists are constrained by this wall which, for historical reasons, they are more likely than not to accept. As refugees from what they conceived to be the 'religious tyrannies' of the Old World, the Protestant colonists who founded the United States in 1776 and won its independence from Britain were opposed to any alliance between state power and religious authority. Churches should be self-governing, autonomous institutions free from taxation and government interference. Nevertheless since all of the Founding Fathers were Protestants, modern fundamentalists can reasonably argue that the United States was founded as a Christian—i.e. Protestant—nation. For them the 'wall of separation' does not mean that the state is atheist or even secular in the fullest sense of the word: merely that it maintains a posture of neutrality towards the different churches or religious denominations. With waves of Catholic migrants from Ireland arriving from the 1830s and Jewish immigration from Eastern and Central Europe from the latter part of the nineteenth century, denominational pluralism was extended beyond what many people (though not Jefferson, who believed in religious freedom 'for the infidel of every denomination') would have imagined during the 1780s.

A landmark Supreme Court decision in 1961 extended to 'secular humanists' (i.e. non-believers) the legal protection accorded to followers of religious faiths. Ironically this is the decision which fundamentalists now use in order to argue that 'secular humanism' qualifies as a religion, for example when values associated with it appear in school curricula. It should therefore be curbed by the state, whose responsibility it is to maintain the 'wall of separation'. American fundamentalists are therefore constrained by the pluralistic religious culture in which they must operate. Rather than forming a religious party aimed at taking over the government, they lobby for power and influence within the Republican Party. Legislative successes at state level have included the reinstitution of daily prayers in some public schools, 'equal time' rules for the teaching of evolution and creation, and the overturning by a dozen or more states of the 1973 Supreme Court *Roe* v. *Wade* judgement repealing state bans on abortion. At the local level fundamentalists have lobbied for the banning of books deemed irreligious from public school libraries or curricula. The banned titles have included such classics as Nathaniel Hawthorne's *The Scarlet Letter*, William Golding's *Lord of the Flies*, and books by Mark Twain, Joseph Conrad, and John Steinbeck, all of which have been seen as promoting the 'religion' of secular humanism by questioning faith in God or portraying religion negatively. These successes, however, have often been reversed by the courts after actions by organizations such as the ACLU and PAW (People for the American Way), a liberal lobby group. At the national level fundamentalism is further constrained by the need to find conservative partners from beyond the ranks of Protestant fundamentalists.

On single issues such as abortion or ERA (the proposed

Equal Rights Amendment for women), fundamentalist lobbying can be efficacious. In the wider political domain, however, American fundamentalists are faced with a dilemma. To collaborate with other conservative groups they must suppress or even abandon their theological objections. As Steve Bruce explains: 'In the world-view which creates the particular reasons conservative Protestants have for resisting modernism, Catholics and Jews are not Christians, and Mormonism is a dangerous cult. But legislative and electoral success requires that fundamentalists work in alliance with such groups and with secular conservatives.'[13] Outside the pro-Life (anti-abortion) and anti-ERA campaigns, which raise gender issues to which all conservative religionists are particularly sensitive, fundamentalists have found little support. Given that religious pluralism is the primary enemy of fundamentalist certainty, this is hardly surprising. In the United States the Constitution, the first in the world to make religious pluralism a central article of faith, is the reef on which the aspirations of 'pure' Protestant fundamentalism seem destined to founder.

To sum up the argument thus far: the F-word originated in the unique context of American religious pluralism and the separation of church and state—conditions which, on the face of it, do not apply elsewhere. However, as has been suggested, the term's particular provenance need not invalidate its application in other contexts. The first time I encountered it in relation to Islam is in a letter written in

family traits ascribed to most fundamentalist movements) Afghani's attitude to modernity was thoroughly ambiguous. Hating imperialism, he nevertheless acknowledged the need for wholescale reforms of the 'Muslim religion', which he saw as decadent, decayed, and corrupt. His spirit is much closer to that of Martin Luther than to, say, a contemporary scriptural literalist such as Jerry Falwell.

The *Strongest Link*, which Afghani founded in Paris with his disciple Muhammad Abduh, was the leading reformist journal of its time. Despite its short duration, it remained an abiding influence on the modernist movement in Islam. The inclusion of Afghani under the 'fundamentalist' label therefore expands our definition not just because Islam is different from Christianity but because what is 'fundamental' to both faiths has been construed differently. Islamic fundamentalism or Islamism, to use an English word that corresponds more closely to the term adopted by contemporary Muslim activists, is not counter-modernist in the way that fundamentalist Christianity has been described as being. Far from challenging the basic premisses of the Enlightenment, the movement launched by Afghani and Abduh in the 1870s, known as the Salafiyya, after the 'pious ancestors' or Prophet's Companions, absorbed the modernist spirit to the point where Abduh broke with Afghani and collaborated with the British power in Egypt to further his reformist agenda. Unlike Christian fundamentalism, Salafism cannot be described as anti-modernist, although the word *salafi* is sometimes used for 'fundamentalist' in Arabic. An alternative Arabic term, *usuli* from *usul* (roots), corresponds more closely to the F-word in English.

A complicating factor here, however, is the specific usage *usuli* has acquired in the religious history of Shiism, the minority tradition in Islam which, like Catholicism, balances adherence to scripture with an emphasis on religious leadership. In the nineteenth century the Shii *ulama* divided into two major schools, the *usulis* and the *akhbaris*. The *usulis* believed in independent *ijtihad*, or reasoning in the interpretation of texts, while the more conservative *akhbaris* relied exclusively on the earlier authorities. Though described in the Western media as a 'fundamentalist', the leader of the 1979 Iranian revolution, Ayatollah Khomeini, belonged to the *usuli* school and upheld its tenets against those of his more conservative or 'fundamentalism', *akhbari* rivals. Though presenting himself as the defender of Islamic 'fundamentalism', Khomeini was a radical innovator in Shii religious and political thought. Despite his frequent denunciations of Marxism, he incorporated a good deal of Marxist thinking into his discourse.

The problems of definition are compounded when so-called Jewish fundamentalism is taken into account. As with Arabic there is no indigenous Hebrew word for 'fundamentalism'. The term usually employed for Jewish extremists by the Israeli media is *yamina dati*, the 'religious right'. Far from rejecting modernity, fundamentalists of the religious right such as Gush Emunim (GE), the Bloc of the Faithful, are religious innovators. Whereas the traditionalist or orthodox groups known as the Haredim regarded the establishment of Israel as an impious pre-empting of the Messiah's role, Gush Emunim and other right-wing religious Zionists see the secular state as a 'stage' towards Redemption. For them the whole Land of Palestine (including the territories captured in the 1967 Arab–Israel war) belongs to the Jewish people and must be held in trust for the coming Messiah. The Haredi groups such as Neturei Karta (NK), the 'Guardians of the City', are much more strict in their adherence to the Halakha, Jewish religious law, than Gush Emunim. The most orthodox or 'fundamentalist' among them do not even recognize the State of Israel: for them the condition of exile is an existential one, fundamental to the very concept of Jewishness. If Jewish 'fundamentalism' can embrace such divergent alternatives as NK and GE, can the term be meaningful or useful?

The question, of course, is theoretical. By now it should be clear that the meanings, or possible applications, of the F-word have strayed far beyond the umbrella of the 'Abrahamic' monotheisms (Judaism, Christianity, and Islam). Sikh 'fundamentalists' took control of the Golden Temple of Amritsar, and when Indira Gandhi sent the troops in, they murdered her in revenge. Hindu 'fundamentalists' demolished the Babri Masjid Mosque at Ayodhya in 1992, believing it to be the site of the birthplace of the deity Rama, setting off communal rioting that led to thousands of deaths. Buddhist monks in Sri Lanka have taken up arms against Tamil separatists, breaking with centuries of pacifism. For their part the Tamils, who pioneered the suicide bomb a decade before Lebanese Shiis and Sunni Palestinians, required their vanguard squads to take an oath to the Hindu god Shiva.

'Fundamentalism' now encompasses many types of activity, not all of them religious. The wing of the Scottish National Party least disposed to cooperate with other parties in the Scottish parliament has been described as 'fundamentalist' by its opponents. Jane Kelsey, a New Zealand economist, describes 'Rogernomics', the free-market policies adopted by the Labour government in the late 1980s and named after the Minister of Finance, Roger Douglas, as 'Economic Fundamentalism'. 'The "funda-mentals" of the programme'—market liberalization and free trade, limited government, a narrow monetarist policy, a deregulated labour market and fiscal restraint—'were systematically embedded against change'. Like holy writ they were assumed to be 'givens', based on common sense and consensus, and beyond challenge.[16] In Germany members of the Green Party who supported Joskha Fischer in joining Gerhard Schroeder's 'Red-Green coali-tion' are described as 'realos' (realists), in contrast to the 'fundis' (fundamentalists) who hold true to the party's ideology of pacifism, opposition to nuclear power, and radical 'Green' environmentalisms. The tension between the two wings was brought to breaking-point when Fischer, as Germany's foreign minister, supported the NATO bombing of Serbia in 1999 while his Green Party colleague, environment minister Jürgen Trittin, was pressured into abandoning a scheme to make auto manufacturers pay for the cost of recycling old cars, and forced to make painful compromises in his plans for phasing out nuclear power.[17]

Similar tensions between ideological purists who stick to the 'fundamentals' of their cause without compromising their principles, and the political realists who argue that real gains can be achieved through bargaining and compromise, exist in all political and cultural movements; indeed they are the very stuff of democratic politics: the energy of political life is released most often when the ideals of party activists are pitted against the realities of power. Virtually every movement, from animal rights to feminism, will embrace a spectrum ranging from uncompromising radicalism or 'extremism' to pragmatic accommodationism. For feminist ultras such as Andrea Dworkin, all penetrative sex is deemed to be rape. For some animal liberationists, every abbattoir, however humane its procedures, is an extermination camp, while in the rhetoric of radical pro-lifers such as Pat Robertson, the 43 million foetuses 'murdered' since *Roe* v. *Wade* are an abomination comparable to the Nazi Holocaust.

At the borders of the semantic field it now occupies, the word fundamentalism strays into 'extremism', 'sectarianism', 'ideological purism'. It seems doubtful, however, if these non-religious uses of the word are analytically useful. There may be some similarities in political and social psychology between, say, anti-abortionists, animal rightists, Green Party activists, Islamist agitators, and the Six Day Creationists who sit on school boards in Kansas or southern California. A reluctance to compromise with one's deeply held principles is an obvious common trait. Such usages, however, seem to me to stray beyond Wittgenstein's 'family resemblances' into something closer to mere analogy. Similarity does not necessarily imply kinship. The genetic bond that defines fundamentalism in its more central, and useful, meaning—the 'fundamentalist DNA', as it were—is sharper and more distinctive than 'extremism'. The original 'Protestant' use of the word anchors it in the responses of individual or collective selfhoods, of personal and group identities, to the scandal or 'shock of the Other'.

Although many religious activists (especially the evangelical movements within Christianity and Islam) believe they have a universal mission to transform or convert the world, all religious traditions must face the problematic of their parochial origins, the embarrassing fact that saviours and prophets uttered divine words in particular languages to relatively small groups of people at particular historical junctures: the late John Lennon was correct in stating that the Beatles were more famous in their time than Jesus was in his. Religious pluralism is an inescapable feature of

2

The Scandal of Difference

The Egyptian historian Abd al-Rahman al-Jabarti (1754–1822) wrote an account of Napoleon's invasion of Egypt in 1798 which perfectly expresses the disdain as well as the fear experienced when a traditional society is exposed to the brutal and outlandish manners of outsiders. Al-Jabarti was no reactionary bigot. He visited the Institut d'Egypte whose outcome—the massive twenty-three-volume *Description de l'Egypte*—is a monument to the science of the Enlightenment, and was impressed by the dedication and scholarship of the savants whom Napoleon had brought with his train. He admitted, after observing experiments conducted by French scientists that 'these are things that the minds of people like us cannot grasp'. But their religion—or lack of it—appalled him. In his mind French irreligion was assimilated to that of the *zindiqs* (Manichaeans) and other enemies of Islam in its earliest phases.

A similar mood, intensified by bitterness at Western

BOX 4

The French follow this rule: great and small, high and low, male and female are all equal. Sometimes they break this rule according to their whims and inclinations or reasoning. Their women do not veil themselves and have no modesty; they do not care whether they uncover their private parts. Whenever a Frenchman has to perform an act of nature he does so wherever he happens to be, even in full view of people, and he goes away as he is, without washing his private parts ... they are materialists, who deny all God's attributes, the Hereafter and Resurrection, and who reject Prophethood and Messengership. They believe that the world was not created, and that the heavenly bodies and occurrences of the Universe are influenced by the movement of the stars, and that nations appear and states decline according to the nature of the conjunctions and the aspects of the moon. Some believe in the transmigration of souls and other fantasies ...

(Abd al-Rahman al-Jabarti, *Napoleon in Egypt*)

support for Israel and the suppression of the Muslim Brotherhood by the Egyptian dictator Gamal 'Abdul Nasser, pervades the writings of the Islamist ideologue Sayyid Qutb. Imprisoned and tortured by Nasser's police and executed in 1966 on what were almost certainly trumped-up charges, Qutb concluded that Muslim society in the Arab world and beyond had ceased to be 'Islamic' having relapsed to the condition of *jahiliya*, the paganism of the 'period of ignorance' that preceded the revelation of Islam. Just as God had authorized Muhammad to fight the Meccan pagans before they eventually submitted to Islam, so Qutb in his prison writings provided the rationale that would later be used to justify the assassination of President Anwar Sadat in October 1981, and, the Islamist attacks on the Egyptian and other nominally Muslim governments, on Western personnel and tourists, and, arguably, the atrocity that killed more than 3,000 people in New York and Washington on 11 September 2001. Though Qutb himself never explicitly advocated violence against individuals, the myth of the *jahiliyya* state, supported by the West, sustains Islamist militants from Algeria to the Philippines.

Humanity today is living in a large brothel! One has only to glance at its press, films, fashion shows, beauty contests, ballrooms, wine bars, and broadcasting stations! Or observe its mad lust for naked flesh, provocative postures, and sick, suggestive statements in literature, the arts and the mass media! And add to all this the system of usury which fuels man's voracity for money and engenders vile methods for its accumulation and investment, in addition to fraud, trickery, and blackmail dressed up in the garb of law.[1]

More than a century and a half separates al-Jabarti's chronicle and the prison writings of Sayyid Qutb. Jabarti was a scholar at the University of al-Azhar trained in the traditional Islamic sciences: the manners and customs of the French disturbed him in the same way that the Taliban, religious students raised in the rural madrasas (seminaries) of northern Pakistan and southern Afghanistan, were shocked by the appearance of unveiled women in the streets of Kabul when they took over the city in 1996. Qutb, by contrast, was a member of the Egyptian intellectual elite. A protégé of the writer Taha Hussein and the poet Abbas Mahmud al-Aqqad, leading lights in Egypt's liberal Western-oriented intelligentsia, he received government funding to study in America, where he attended universities in Washington DC, Colorado, and California. It was exposure to Western (particularly American) culture, not ignorance, that led to his revulsion. His is the paradigmatic case of the 'born-again' Muslim who having adopted or absorbed many modern or foreign influences makes a show of discarding them in his search for personal identity and cultural authenticity. The term fundamentalist may be appropriate, but in Qutb's case it is still problematic. Far from espousing received theological certainties or defending 'Muslim society' against foreign encroachments, Qutb's understanding of Islam seems almost Kierkegaardian in its individualism: his 'authentic' Muslim is one who espouses a very modern kind of revolution against the deification of men, against injustice, and against political, economic, racial and religious prejudice.[2]

Behind both these responses, Jabarti's and Qutb's, lies a particularly Islamic response to the loss of cultural hegemony. Elsewhere I have suggested that Islam, whose formative institutions were created during a period of historic triumph, is 'programmed for victory'. Outside the Shii minority tradition which, like Christianity, has myths and theologies for dealing with failure, Islam has been a triumphalist faith. Non-Muslims were tolerated on condition that they accepted or recognized their subordinate status. Jabarti's perplexity and Qutb's rage are both responses to the scandalous fact that the Enlightenment, with all the consequences it held for religious decline, occurred not in the Muslim world, whose scientific and humanistic culture prepared the ground for it, but in the West, a barbarous and, to Muslim minds, backward region whose primitive faith had been superseded by Islam, God's final revelation.

The crisis that normative Islam faces in its relation with the contemporary world is partly historical. It flows from the contradiction between the collective memory of the triumphal progress of Muhammad's original movement and the conquests of his immediate successors, and the experience of recent political failure during the colonial and post-colonial periods, when most of the Islamic world came under Western political, cultural, and commercial domination. Outside the Arabian peninsular, most of the world that had lived and prospered for centuries under the imperial faith of Islam became subject to European imperialism in some form, prompting reformers such as Sayyid Ahmed Khan in India and Muhammad Abduh in

Egypt to ally themselves to European power in order to try to accommodate the scientific and humanistic knowledge of the West with the cultural norms of Islam. The result was a de facto separation of religious and secular culture contrary to the stated nostrums of Islamic tradition, which did not acknowledge a formal distinction between 'religion' and 'the world' (Arabic *din wa dunya*). Modernization (including political modernization) proceeded along the secular path, whilst religion remained for the most part in the custody of traditionalist *ulama* who (unlike their counterparts in Protestant seminaries) avoided the challenge (posed by Jamal al-Din al-Afghani, Muhammad Abduh, and Sayyid Ahmad Khan) of modernizing the religion from within.

The fundamentalist impulse in Islam thus takes a different form from its counterpart in Protestant Christianity, where the struggle between fundamentalism and liberalism was for the most part waged inside the churches and the teaching institutions that served them. In the majority Sunni tradition it is driven mainly by the secular elites, beneficiaries of modern scientific and technical educations, who wish to reintegrate the religious, cultural, and political life of their societies along Islamic lines: the shorthand for this aspiration is the 'restoration of the Sharia' (Islamic law). Scholars make a distinction between those Islamists who put more emphasis on voluntary Islamization 'from below', through preaching, the building or taking-over of state mosques, the creation of charit-

been God-fearing Christians, and more recently to the world-view of small-town America epitomized by Jerry Falwell's popular television show, the *Old Time Gospel Hour*. Hindu and Jewish fundamentalists also subscribe to myths of a golden age: Hindus venerate the Kingdom of Ayodhya, whose ruler Lord Rama they wish to 'restore' to his temple on the site of the Babri Masjid—the mosque built by Babur, the first Moghul conqueror, which militants demolished in 1992. Some Jewish fundamentalists hark back to the era of David, and to Solomon, builder of the First Temple in Jerusalem. Its restoration, like that of Ayodhya, would necessitate the destruction of a Muslim shrine—in this case the Dome of the Rock from where Muhammad is supposed to have ascended to heaven. Others, such as the Neturei Karta ('Guardians of the City'), look back to a more recent era. Wearing the frock coats, broad-brimmed hats, and ringlets of the eighteenth-century *shtetels* of Eastern Europe, they seek to preserve the enclave culture of the ghettos, the close-knit, Halakha-governed, autonomous communities prior to the Jewish Enlightenment, before the process of modernization and secularization began. Orthodox Jewish groups which strictly observe the Halakha had been conditioned by a 'fundamentalist' refusal to abandon the condition of exile long before anti-Semitic persecutions drove them back into the ghettos of Eastern Europe. Transplanted to Palestine after the Holocaust by necessity rather than choice, their attitudes towards the secular Zionist state range from

BOX 5

The encounter of the world faiths is still only just beginning, even today. There are many historical and sociological reasons for the delay. Chief among them, no doubt, is the understandable belief that one's own tradition, after long centuries of development and diversification, contains within itself resources varied enough to meet the needs of all types of individual. This argument for staying within one's own camp is, however, vulnerable to something that we might call 'religion-shock' on the analogy of culture-shock. Religion-shock occurs when someone who is a strong and sincere believer in his own faith confronts, without evasion and without being able to explain it away, the reality of an entirely different form of faith, and faces the consequent challenge to his own deepest assumptions.

(Don Cupitt, *The Sea of Faith*)

formal non-recognition to de facto collaboration. Most of the Haredim accept that it is pointless to try to impose the Halakha on the rest of society: 'the "state of the Jews" can become a "Jewish state" only when the Messiah comes.' The attitude corresponds to that of the premillennial Protestants, who see themselves as the saved remnant of humanity pending the Return of Jesus. Since the condition of exile is an existential one, an alienation from the godhead which cannot be overcome by human action, some of the Haredim do not even recognize Israel as the Jewish homeland, although, pragmatically, they have made their accommodations with it. Instead they reconfigure themselves as the real 'Jews', now in 'exile' within the secular Zionist state. Gush Emunim, by contrast, are future-oriented: like some radical Islamists and post-millennial Protestants, they seek to establish utopian society based on the rule of God.

In all such cases the vision is monocultural. The group or enclave it supports rejects the pluralism and diversity which constitute one the defining characteristics of the modern world. Modernity pluralizes, introducing choices (including religious choices) where none existed before. Before modern forms of travel and communications made people living in different cultural systems aware of each other, most people assumed that their own way of life or system of beliefs were the norm. The same considerations applied to social life and industrial activity. 'Where there used to be one or two institutions, there are now fifty; where there used to be one or two programs in a particular area of human life, there are now fifty.' As Steve Bruce, following Peter Berger, stresses, in the pre-modern world of limited technology the one available tool was accompanied by a belief in the single way of doing things. 'One employs this tool, for a particular purpose and no other. One dresses in this particular way and no other. A traditional society is one in which the great part of human activity is governed by such clear-cut prescriptions.'[3]

For pre-modern Judaism the barriers created by religious identity and external hostility were mutually reinforcing. Similarly, pre-modern Catholic Christianity enforced strict religious conformity, and it was only after centuries of conflict between Catholics and Protestants (and within Protestantism)—conflicts that assisted the emergence of the Enlightenment—that a modus vivendi between the two faiths was achieved. Pockets of religious intolerance still survive in Northern Ireland, where political differences between republicans and loyalists are buttressed by competing religious identities: virtually all republicans are Catholic, all loyalists are Protestant. In the United States explicit anti-Catholicism in the Protestant nativist and 'know-nothing' movements lasted well into the twentieth century, as did religious anti-Semitism (or Judaeophobia).

Compared to pre-Enlightenment Christendom, the record of Islam is impressive. Pre-modern Islam formally tolerated Jews and Christians as *dhimmis* or peoples of the book entitled to Muslim protection, a status later extended to Zoroastrianism, Hinduism, and other 'scriptural' religions. Protection, however, is not the same as full religious tolerance. The *dhimmis* were not accorded legal equality and in most Islamic societies rules affecting marriage, legal testimony, house construction, costume, and animal transport pointedly emphasized their inferior social status. Islamists in Egypt, Pakistan, and Bangladesh (among other countries) have demanded the restoration of *dhimmi* status to non-Muslims (including Coptic Christians and Hindus), and to Muslim groups they consider heretical, which would limit their rights as full citizens.

Though fundamentalists, as we shall see, have not been slow to embrace such aspects of modernity as they find congenial—especially modern technologies (including radio, television, electronics, and armaments) they consider helpful to their cause—they do not or cannot fully accept religious pluralism. Islamist extremists in Upper Egypt have tried to extract the *jizya* tax from the Christian Coptic minority—a payment that would symbolize their inferior status. The Hindu 'fundamentalists' of the BJP (Bharatiya Janata Party) and RSS (Rashtriya Svayamsevak Sangh, or 'national union of volunteers') believe that Indian nationhood must be based on 'caste'—the social categories recognized in classical Hinduism, thus excluding Muslims, Sikhs, Christians, tribal peoples, and even non-resident Indians (NRIs) from their notion of Indian identity. Jewish fundamentalists tend to be narrower in their definitions of what constitutes Jewish identity than secular Zionists. The extremists among them such as Baruch Goldstein, who killed some thirty Arab worshippers at the Tomb of the Patriarchs in Hebron in 1994, and his mentor, Rabbi Meir Kahane, held views about Arabs that were remarkably similar to Adolf Hitler's views about the Jews. Premillennial Protestants believe that following the return of Christ to earth, which is imminent, those who accept the Messiah (i.e. born-again Christians), including 144,000 'righteous' Jews, will be 'raptured' into Heaven, while the unrighteous majority (including nominal Christians and 'unsaved' members of other religious traditions), will perish miserably. Indeed for many conservative Protestants, Catholics are not Christians, Episcopalians and Unitarians are atheists, Mormonism is a dangerous cult, while Hinduism, Buddhism, and other non-Western religions are Satanic. As for Islam, Jerry Falwell spoke for many American evangelicals after 9/11: 'Mohammed was a terrorist.'[4]

In practice some tactical accommodations with pluralism may be necessary, and fundamentalists who want to pursue a political agenda (such as banning abortion or blocking the constitutional amendment guaranteeing equal rights for women) have found it expedient to collaborate with religious groups they regard as heretical. In principle, however, the commands of God as understood by the faithful are non-negotiable, absolute, and unconditional. For Jerry Falwell all who fail—after hearing it—to accept the Christian gospel are doomed; in the Islamist view the same goes for the Koran and teachings of Muhammad.

Since God is reported to have said different things to the numerous individuals claiming to speak on his behalf, belief in the truth held by one tradition necessarily excludes all others. This is especially so in the Abrahamic tradition of Western monotheism, where confessions are deemed to be exclusive: in the mainstream, orthodox versions of these faiths one cannot be a Muslim and a Christian, or a Christian and a Jew. In a globalized culture where religions are in daily contact with their competitors,

BOX 6

The Quran does not claim that Islam is the true compendium of rites and rituals, and metaphysical beliefs and concepts, or that it is the proper form of religious (as the word religion is nowadays understood in Western terminology) attitude of thought and action for the individual. Nor does it say that Islam is the true way of life for the people of Arabia, or for the people of any particular country or for the people preceding any particular age (say, the Industrial Revolution), No! Very explicitly, for the entire human race, there is only one way of life which is Right in the eyes of God and that is al-Islam.

(Sayyid Abu Ala Mawdudi, *The Religion of Truth*)

denial of pluralism is a recipe for conflict. Yet acceptance of pluralism relativizes truth. Once it is allowed that there are different paths to truth a person's religious allegiance becomes a matter of choice, and choice is the enemy of absolutism. Fundamentalism is one response to the crisis of faith brought about by awareness of differences. As Clifford Geertz once put it: 'From now on no one will leave anyone else alone.'[5] When traditional cultures no longer feel 'left alone' or when they want to intrude on 'the other' of whom they become aware, tradition ceases to be tradition in the traditional sense of the word.

As Steve Bruce argues, even if the contents of competing visions are rejected, the constant evidence that there are many alternative visions cannot be ignored. Initially religious competitors can be stigmatized by invoking invidious stereotypes—'Catholicism is the creed of Rome and rebellion; unitarianism and humanism are the creeds of degenerate upper classes; enthusiastic pentecostalism is the faith of the lumpen proletariat.' Such stereotyping, however, is inevitably subject to the law of diminishing returns. 'When there is so much variation in and across all social strata, even the most successful techniques for cognitive insulation fail to disguise the reality of choice.'[6]

Religious pluralism, by which I mean the policy of granting public recognition to more than one religious tradition, is as integral to modernity as cars, aeroplanes, television, and the internet: indeed it is a consequence of a world where everyone is increasingly aware of everyone else, where 'no one leaves anyone else alone'. Since the Reformation broke the monopoly of the Roman Catholic Church, pluralism has been institutionalized in the West, and although the process was a gradual one (with Catholics in Britain, for example, only granted the vote in the nineteenth century) the spread of pluralism has become unstoppable. The wars of religion in Germany, culminating in the Peace of Westphalia (1648), established pluralism under the principle *cuius regio, eius religio*—'religion belongs to the ruler'. This was far from being toleration: rulers retained the right to impose their religion on their subjects, with Catholics persecuted in Protestant domains, and vice versa. But it marked an irrevocable step towards toleration. Boundaries being porous, states acquired minorities. Though conformity was rigorously enforced in countries such as France, England, and Spain, religious uniformity proved unsustainable. Toleration, the political consequence of the Reformation's challenge to the Church's monopoly, became a prerequisite of Enlightenment thought, an 'apanage of reason', as Voltaire would call it. 'Superstition and dogma', originally the target of Protestants, became the bugbears of all Enlightenment thinkers. Already for Pierre Bayle, writing in the 1690s, God was 'too benevolent a being to be the author of anything so pernicious as the revealed religions which carry in themselves the inexterminable seeds of war, slaughter and injustice'.[7] By the mid-eighteenth century the deists had assimilated God to pure reason, decoupling the deity from the religions that claimed to speak for him.

Protestant America, founded by religious refugees from Europe, developed its own distinctive style of pluralism known as denominationalism, becoming after the revolution the first polity in the world with an explicit guarantee of religious freedom. (The French and Russian revolutions, by contrast, were violently anti-religious in their initial phases.) The US Constitution built a 'wall of separation' between church and state that was supposed to prevent any one tradition or 'denomination' from exercising state power over the others. American churches are privileged self-governing enclaves. They are self-financing, though as non-profit corporations they benefit from negative subsidies since their earnings are free from tax (though there are grey areas such as rents and property where their tax-exempt status is hotly contested by government). In practice the 'divine supermarket' brought into being by religious deregulation enabled the free churches such as Baptists and Methodists (minorities in Europe) to expand more rapidly than the more tightly controlled churches such as the Anglicans, Congregationalists, or Presbyterians. The latter had exercised state control during the colonial period with each of the Thirteen Colonies having its own establishment—Massachusetts was Congregationalist, New York Presbyterian, Maryland Catholic, Virginia Anglican, and so forth. As Will Herberg observed half a century ago, the denomination is a uniquely American creation. It is 'the non-conformist sect become central and normative'. It differs from the European idea of the Church 'in that it would never claim to be the national institution', but it also differs from the sect in being 'socially established, thoroughly institutionalised and nuclear to the society in which it is found'.[8] In American Christendom the 'fringe' becomes the centre. Even the Roman Catholic Church became subject to the democratizing effects of denominationalism, as Alex de Tocqueville noted on his famous visit to the United States in 1825.

In Europe religious toleration and the secularization of government occurred more gradually, with historic state churches retaining a degree of institutional monopoly. In Germany and Scandinavia churches are subsidized out of taxation; in Britain the established churches (Anglican in England and Wales, Presbyterian in Scotland) are the beneficiaries of large endowments built up over centuries. The Catholic Church in France, Italy, and Spain is formally separate from the state (with religion in France limited, since 1905, to the private sphere) but it nevertheless retains a powerful institutional presence through its educational establishments and the symbolism of its architecture. Paradoxically, the closer connections between church and state in Europe seem to have facilitated the secularization of society, with regular church attendance (as distinct from formal church membership) in rapid decline in most European countries. In the United States, by contrast, deregulation, and the ensuing competition between churches, the absence of an anti-clerical tradition and the cultural presence of Protestantism as a 'civil religion' have combined to make Christianity—the religion of 86 per cent of the population—an important element in public life, despite (or perhaps because of) disestablishment. In contrast to Europe, where many of the educational, pastoral, and social functions once performed by the Church have been taken over by state authorities, America's churches still dispose of significant social power. Under certain conditions that power can become political.

At the same time, conservative Christians (including some Catholics and Mormons) as well as some Jews have felt themselves to be increasingly under attack as the state has encroached upon areas previously considered to be the preserve of religious communities. Throughout the United States—and not just in the 'Bible Belt' of Texas and the Old South—fundamentalists have taken action in defence of their idea of a Christian America. Successive court decisions, usually backed by mainstream liberal denominations, have outlawed racial segregation, discrimination against women, racial minorities, and homosexuals. Prayer has been banned in publicly funded schools in furtherance of church–state separation and non-Christians of all persuasions, including outright atheists and 'secular humanists', have been accorded the legal protections the constitution guarantees.

When these and many other developments threatened what they saw as their 'freedom', fundamentalists were moved to 'fight back' to defend their idea of a Christian America. In their view the pluralism permitted under the Constitution was implicitly limited to Protestant Christianity; and while it might be stretched to include Jews and Catholics, the idea that 'Satanic' Hindus and outright atheists could benefit from laws intended to preserve denominational pluralism within the Judaeo-Christian fold was anathema.

To the scandal of difference one should add the scandal of social and behavioural change. As Bruce explains in the American context, 'One need not follow fundamentalists in their uncritical attitude to the past, their blanket condemnation of the present, nor in their explanation of the ways in which the world has changed to accept that divorce is now common, as is drug addiction, that homosexuality is accepted in many circles as an alternative lifestyle, that "housewife" is a devalued status, that the separation of church and state (once interpreted as denominational neutrality) is now taken to imply secularity, and so on.' He concludes that the changes that have been promoted and welcomed by atheists, feminists, racial minorities, and liberals 'have fundamentally altered the moral, social and political culture of America and moved it away from the standards and practices that fundamentalists regard as biblical'.[9]

From their own perspective Christian fundamentalists may have a point. State legislation, for example in education, has become increasingly intrusive. First public schools were desegregated, with 'busing' introduced to assist racial integration. When conservatives responded by establishing their own independent Christian schools, the state intervened by removing their tax-exempt status if they appeared segregationist. It supported state legislatures which required the licensing even of independent schools. In the media religious conservatives of all persuasions experienced the 'intrusion' of 'secular humanism' or 'Godless' values in such areas as the public acceptance of nudity, homosexuality, sex outside marriage, and the termination of pregnancies.

In other countries also, the reactions generated by similar changes can be seen as a response to the increasing intrusiveness on the part of the state. In traditional Islamic societies before the colonial intervention in the nineteenth century, the state had a 'watchdog' role that allowed civil society to manage itself with a minimum of political interference. Formally the Islamic ruler, the Sultan or 'authority', was subject to the rule of Islamic law, although in practice his governance could be supplemented by royal decrees. Though the Sultan appointed the judges, the law was interpreted and administered by the *ulama*, a class of literate scholars often tied by family links to the merchant class. Though often thought of as harsh by modern standards because of the use of corporal punishments for certain categories of crime, the thrust of the law was not so much to uphold the state as to maintain social harmony by mediating between contending parties. Challenged by the rising power of the European nations, reforming autocrats used their prerogative powers to whittle away the autonomy of civil society in Muslim lands. Their modern successors, in most cases, have continued along the same path. In the post-colonial era the Muslim world has seen a progressive intrusion of the state into areas hitherto reserved for voluntary activity, including education, social welfare, industrial production, and even the 'sacred' arena of family life. In the Arab world especially, nationalist regimes enthusiastically adopted the Marxist model imported from Eastern Europe where the single party state became the primary agency for political, economic, and social mobilization, ruling by a combination of state patronage and police repression.

Though the Jewish example differs significantly, similar patterns can still be observed. The Zionist movement which culminated in the creation of Israel in 1948 was dominated by secular intellectuals from its beginnings in Europe. Throughout most of the half-century of Israel's existence the prevailing tone has been secular and democratic. The religious parties represented in the Knesset (the Israeli parliament) have extracted concessions from successive governments on state funding for religious education, exemptions from military service for yeshiva (seminary) students, marriage and divorce and other questions of personal status, including the problematic question of Jewish identity (the 'Who is a Jew' controversy). For a religious tradition forged during centuries of exile, however, a state in which Jews are a majority poses special problems. In some cases the 'minority syndrome' is so strong that the faithful redesignate themselves as the real or authentic Jews in contradistinction to the 'gentile' majority. Far from permitting a relaxation of the Halakhic rules, customs formulated under the conditions of exile are adhered to as rigidly as they were in the diaspora.

One can discern in such paradoxes the inertia or inherent conservatism underpinning group identities where continuity is sustained through repetition. Ulster Protestants re-enact and ritualize the events to which they believe they owe their religious 'liberty'—the Battle of the Boyne on 12 July, the closing of the Gates of Londonderry by the Apprentice Boys in 1689. Muslim settlers in

Surinam (formerly Dutch Guyana) brought from Java in the nineteenth century still pray westwards towards Mecca, instead of facing east, as their new location should require. Fundamentalist movements may be grounded emotionally in communities forged under minority conditions, where the sense of embattlement, of being an island of virtue or faith in a sea of ignorance or sin, is strong. But unlike sects such as the Amish, who may be happy to be left alone in horse-drawn, zipper-free isolation, the fundamentalism with which we are primarily concerned has broader ambitions. Seldom content with defending its minority status against the onslaughts of a pluralistic, secular world, it strives to 'fight back' by exercising power, directly or indirectly. The encroachments of modernity through state power and state bureaucracies are pervasive and continuous and a constant challenge to all religious traditions. For the activist fundamentalist (as distinct from the passive traditionalist) the quest for salvation cannot be realized by withdrawing into a cultural enclave.

3

The Snares of Literalism

Words strain,
Crack and sometimes break, under the burden,
Under the tension, slip, slide, perish,
Decay with imprecision, will not stay in place,
Will not stay still.

(T. S. Eliot, 'Burnt Norton')

Fundamentalists everywhere tend towards a literalist interpretation of the texts they revere. A survey by the Gallup organization in 1980 found that 40 per cent of the American public claimed to believe that the Bible is the 'actual word of God and is to be taken literally, word for word'.[1] This attitude, of course, is far from being a recent phenomenon. As George Dollar of Bob Jones University put it in his *History of Fundamentalism in America*, 'historic fundamentalism is the literal exposition of all the affirmation and attitudes of the Bible and the militant exposure of all non-Biblical affirmation and attitudes'.[2]

Similarly most orthodox Muslims, not just those described as Islamists or militants, are fundamentalist in the sense that they take the Koran to be the literal Word of God, as dictated to the Prophet Muhammad through the agency of the Angel Gabriel (Jibreel). Since it was assembled by the Third Caliph Uthman (reigned 644–656 CE) the text is considered perfect, complete, and unalterable. For conservative Muslim scholars as for radical fundamentalists, the style of historical criticism that sees the language of revelation as a human construct reflecting the knowledge and prejudice of its time is anathema. The Egyptian academic Nasr Abu Zaid, who ventured to use modern literary critical methodology in his approach to the Koran, was forced into exile; 'higher criticism' of the Koran, where the text is deconstructed in accordance with methods developed by biblical scholars since the eighteenth century, is still very largely confined to scholars who are not Muslims. Examples include the work of John Wansbrough, Patricia Crone, and Gerald Hawting, Western scholars of Islam who do not accept the traditional view of its origins as related in the earliest texts.

There is more to 'literalism', however, than appears at first sight. A straightforward definition means reading the text at its plainest, most obvious. For some fundamentalists that would mean, for example, that when the Bible, in Genesis 1, tells us that God created the world in six days and rested on the seventh, the word 'day' corresponds to the usual dictionary definition of a twenty-four-hour period (or perhaps a twelve-hour period in which 'day' is con-

BOX 7

Even if fundamentalists sometimes say that they take the Bible literally, the facts of fundamentalist interpretation show that this is not so. What fundamentalists insist on is not that the Bible must be taken literally but that it must be so interpreted as to avoid any admission that it contains any kind of error. In order to avoid imputing error to the Bible, fundamentalists twist and turn back and forward between literal and non-literal interpretation … What they mean and are constantly interpreted as meaning, is that the Bible contains no error of any kind—not only theological error, but error in any sort of historical, geographical or scientific fact …

(James Barr, *Fundamentalism*)

trasted with 'night'). Some fundamentalist theologians, however, retreat from this definition by arguing that since night and day as experienced by humans are caused by the earth turning on its axis, the 'days' prior to the creation can be understood to mean geological ages. In support of this they cite a verse from Psalm 90: 'a thousand years in Thy sight are like yesterday', which shows that 'in other parts of scripture the word "day" is employed figuratively of a time of undefined length'.[3] The issue, according to the liberal theologian James Barr, is not so much about literalism as *inerrancy*.

At its starkest, literalism means that the letter or exact wording of a text carries the whole weight of its meaning, excluding any unmentioned or extraneous data. An example is a well-known case in British law. A wealthy Scot who lived in Edinburgh named in his will the National Society for the Prevention of Cruelty to Children (NSPCC) rather than the Scottish NSPCC, an entirely different charity—although he had shown some interest in the latter during his lifetime. Despite the arguments of the Scottish charity's lawyers that the NSPCC, based in London, was unknown to the benefactor, the Law Lords awarded the legacy to the London society on the ground that there was no explicit indication of the benefactor's intention to leave it to the Scottish society.[4]

Sacred texts, however, rarely lend themselves to mechanical literalism in this way. Fundamentalists in general avoid addressing ambiguities of language by arguing that the plain meanings of scriptures are an integral part of their moralizing purpose. Thus the nineteenth-century Christian theologian T. H. Horne insisted that 'in common life, no prudent or conscientious person, who either commits his sentiments to writing or utters anything, intends that a diversity of meanings should be attached to what he writes or says; and consequently, neither his readers, nor those who hear him, affix to it any other than the true and obvious sense'.[5] For fundamentalists the same is supposed to apply, *a fortiori*, to the writers of scripture inspired by the Holy Spirit (or, in the case of Islam, to the words of the Koran dictated to Muhammad by God by the agency of the angel).

Literalism, however, contains pitfalls of its own making. The understanding of texts in their literal sense—as distinct from their mythical or allegorical meanings—may open those very floodgates of textual criticism to which fundamentalists are most adamantly opposed. As Barr points out, the contradictions and anomalies in the Bible were spotted not by scholars primarily concerned with its mythological or allegorical meanings, but by 'literalists' who paid detailed attention to the plain meanings of the texts.

Modern textual criticism began with the Pentateuch, the first five books of the Old Testament, whose authorship was attributed to Moses, though he appears as a character in them, and, among other anomalies, the narrative includes the account of his death. The stories in the Pentateuch contain many contradictions, anomalies, overlappings, and 'doublets' (the same story told with different details) from which scholars eventually concluded that the text was constructed out of four separate sources known by the letters J, E, D, and P. Medieval Jewish and Christian commentators explained such anomalies by arguing that as a Prophet of God Moses would have had knowledge of things that were hidden to others. In the eleventh century CE Isaac ibn Yashush, Jewish physician to one of the Muslim rulers in Spain, pointed out that the list of Edomite kings in Genesis 36 named several who lived long after Moses was supposed to have died. Thereafter early modern sceptics, including Thomas Hobbes and Baruch

Spinoza, began to note details that seemed inconsistent with Mosaic authorship. From the nineteenth century modern source criticism saw a consensus developing around the theme of multiple authorship of the Penta-teuch. 'At present ... there is hardly a biblical scholar in the world actively working on the problem who would claim that the Five Books of Moses were written by Moses—or by any one person.'[6] Similar findings apply to other Old Testament books, while textual criticism has revealed in the New Testament a mosaic or patchwork of materials from which the canon containing the Four Gospels, the Acts of the Apostles, the Epistles of Paul and Peter, and the Book of Revelation were constructed.

Barr draws attention to the 'absurd lack of proportion between the things that are religiously important to funda-mentalists and the arguments about scripture by which they seek to guarantee them'. In what way, he asks, would the religious life be imperilled, if it were to be believed that the book named after the prophet Isaiah were written by a series of other prophets, or if Deuteronomy were known to have been written not by Moses but many centuries after his death, or if it was thought that the Epistle to Titus were not written by St Paul? He concludes that there is 'absolutely nothing in the characteristic evangelical reli-gious pattern that would necessarily be imperiled if these elementary concepts of biblical criticism were to be accepted'.[7]

The *problématique* of literalist interpretation lies in the assumption that words can be understood separately from the hearer or reader's presuppositions about their context, meaning, or intent. 'Calling a spade a spade' is only meaningful when one is familiar with a certain type of garden tool—one that is already being superseded by small tractors and other power-driven machines. The original auditors of the scriptures or their earliest readers were people of their times. However hard fundamentalists try to resist the thrust of historical criticism, by insisting that God's Word is Timeless and Eternal, the facts alluded to in the scriptures can only be defended, as Barr points out, by shifting the ground away from literalism and towards inerrancy.

Thus Maurice Bucaille, in a book popular with Islamic fundamentalists, claims that the Koran contains references to many scientific facts of recent discovery, such as atoms, particles, and viruses.[8] The perils of 'pure' literalism are illustrated by the famous example of Sheikh Abdullah bin Baz, the former chief mufti of Saudi Arabia, who on the basis of Koranic references to the 'seven heavens' of the Ptolemaic system, threatened to excommunicate anyone subscribing to the Copernican cosmology that replaced it in the seventeenth century. Embarrassed by the scandal occasioned by the worthy sheikh's views, which the Egyptian press took pleasure in publicizing, most Islamists interpret the 'seven heavens' symbolically.

In one way the sheikh's *fatwa* illustrates a benchmark in the transition from traditionalism to fundamentalism, the point where traditionalism becomes self-consciously reactive. Whereas the true traditionalist does not know he is a traditionalist, the fundamentalist is forced by the logic of his desire to defend tradition into making strategic selections. Textual anomalies are either denied, or subsumed into the hermeneutics of inerrancy, where the burden of proof is shifted from God to humanity. They can then be explained as errors of human understanding, rather than flaws in the text itself.

Bin Baz's insistence *after* the Copernican revolution that the sun goes round the earth is not really the same as that of the pre-Copernican astronomers. He has in fact taken up an attitude to evidence which the pre-Copernicans had not been able to consider, and which would in all reasonable probability have caused them to modify their Ptolemaic views, if they had had access to it.[9] By a similar logic, the doctrine of inerrancy finesses the problem of literalism. An obvious example lies in the miracle stories that abound in the Old and New Testaments. Far from taking the medieval or traditionalist view of miracles, according to which God intervenes in natural processes by causing waters to rise up, or the sun to stand still, fundamentalist commentators tend to rationalize miracles by suggesting that they accord with natural processes. While not denying the possibility of miracles in principle, they tend to de-emphasize them in fact.

In the Old Testament Joshua leads the Children of Israel across the Jordan when the river is in full flood after telling them that the moment the priests carrying the Ark of the Covenant set foot in the waters of the sacred river 'the water coming down from upstream will stand piled up like a bank or heap'; and so it came to pass. According to the New English Bible the moment the priests stepped into the water 'it piled up like a bank for a long way back, as far as Adam, a town near Zarethan'.[10] A conservative commentator, Hugh J. Blair, points to an 'interesting parallel' in the account of an Arab historian who in 1266 described how the bed of the Jordan was left dry for several hours after a landslide near Tel el-Damiya, 'which many experts have identified with Adam'. 'In 1927', he continues, 'an earthquake caused the west bank to collapse near the location of Adam, and the Jordan was dammed up for more than twenty-one hours.'[11] Here, as in many other instances, the miracle is given a naturalizing and rationalizing explanation.

New Testament miracles may similarly be rationalized by conservative commentators. The star which guides the Magi to the stable where Jesus was born in Matthew 2 'may have been the close conjunction of Jupiter and Saturn in 7 BC', according to R. E. Nixon in *The New Bible Commentary Revised*.[12] The same commentator even hints at, before rejecting, the possibility that the story of Jesus' walking on the sea in Matthew 14: 25 is really a mistranslation for 'on the sea shore'—a reading which would totally undermine the story's religious significance.[13]

Some Islamic fundamentalist commentators also shy

away from strict literalism in their interpretations of the Koran. Sayyid Qutb, the most influential of modern Sunni theorists in the Arab world, is best known for redefining the concept of *jahiliya*, the 'age of ignorance' before the coming of Islam, in terms of the modern state, thereby de-legitimizing it. Executed for his participation in an alleged plot to overthrow President Gamal Abdul Nasser in 1966, Qutb achieved a kind of posthumous revenge on the 'infidel' government which martyred him: his resurrection of the writings of the thirteenth-century Hanbali scholar Ibn Taymiyya contributed indirectly to the murder of President Anwar Sadat in 1981. But while doubtless a 'militant', perhaps even an 'extremist', in his implacable hostility to the *jahiliya* state, Qutb was hardly fundamentalist in the sense of taking a literalistic view of scripture.

The thirty-volume commentary on the Koran Qutb wrote in prison is full of a rationalist exegesis extolling the creative power of God in nature, in a manner somewhat reminiscent of *Paley's Evidences*. In it Qutb retreats significantly from the rationalism of Muhammad Abduh, the Islamic reformer who produced a modernizing exegesis of the Koran. For example in his commentary on the Koranic story of the miraculous defeat of an Abyssinian army besieging Mecca by the flock of birds armed with stones, Qutb cites Abduh's opinion that the creatures in question were really flies or mosquitoes which infected the invaders with disease (an interpretation which, like Nixon and

Blair's, suggests that divine intervention accords with natural processes).

Qutb, however, does not insist on a more visibly supernatural intervention: he merely leaves the question open, contrasting Abduh's rationalizing treatment with the much more colourful medieval versions, pointing out that Abduh and his disciples showed a 'strong desire' in their commentaries to reduce the number of miracles in the Koran. It may be, Qutb concludes, that they have gone too far in de-emphasizing Allah's limitless capacity to transcend the laws of nature: the divine will may well have been executed by supernatural means. At the same time Qutb is careful to insist that Muslims should guard themselves against unwarranted superstitions.

Qutb's position is consistent with that of several modern Muslim writers who, like liberal Protestants, have accepted Darwinian evolution as 'God's way of doing things'. The 'father of Islamic fundamentalism', Jamal al-Din al-Afghani, is an influential exception: in 1881 he explicitly attacked Darwinism in his famous tract, entitled *The Refutation of Materialists*. But as the Arab scholar Adel Ziadat points out, Afghani was only vaguely familiar with Darwin's ideas, and subsequent Muslim writers have generally taken a more liberal view. There are numerous passages in the Koran extolling Allah's creative power which Muslim scholars could cite as being consistent with evolutionary theory: for example in 22: 5 Allah tells Muhammad, 'We have created you [i.e. humanity] from

BOX 8

One group of materialists decided that the germs of all species, especially animals, are identical, that there is no difference between them and that the species also have no essential distinction. Therefore, they said, those germs transferred from one species to another and changed from one form to another through the demands of time and place, according to need and moved by external forces ... The leader of this school is Darwin. He wrote a book stating that man descends from the monkey, and that in the course of successive centuries as a result of external impulses he changed until he reached the stage of the orang-utan. From that form he rose to the earliest human degree, which was the race of cannibals and other Negroes. Then some men rose and reached a position on a higher plane than that of the Negroes, the plane of Caucasian man.

(Jamal al-Din al-Afghani, in *An Islamic Response to Imperialism*)

dust, then from sperm, then from a little lump of flesh formed and unformed, that we may make it clear for you.'[14] Following the example of Muhammad Abduh, Muslim writers tended to read modern scientific ideas into the Koran, while asserting that such concepts really had Islamic roots and that nothing in the divine text contradicted them. In the realm of scientific thought generally textual inerrancy has been easier to defend in the Koran than in the Bible.

'We can only seek God in His Word' wrote Jean Calvin, 'nor think of Him otherwise than according to the Word.' The cult of the text was always implicit in Protestantism, where biblical authority outweighed the 'cumulative tradition' represented by the teaching and authority of the Catholic Church. Here an important question arises: Can Catholics be fundamentalists? The F-word originated with Protestant evangelicals protesting at the encroachments of liberal theology: what of conservative Catholics who hold similar views? The problem is complicated, however, by a defining feature of Catholicism that is in direct contrast to the cult of the text to be found in the Protestant and mainstream Islamic traditions: loyalty to the Church as an institution embodying a tradition of religious authority as important as scripture itself. The Catholic equivalent of fundamentalism is known as *intégrisme* in French, integralism in German and English. Until quite recently the term *fondamentalisme* was not even found in French dictionaries to refer to a religious doctrine. Structurally, integralism is the equivalent of fundamentalism. It cares less, however, for a 'literalism of the book' than for what one Jesuit scholar calls 'papal fundamentalism: a literal, ahistorical and nonhermeneutical reading of papal pronouncements, even papal obiter dicta, as a bulwark against the tides of relativism, the claims of science, and the inroads of modernity'.[15] A family resemblance to integralism may be found in other religious traditions that emphasize the integrity, or divine quality, of religious leadership—for example, among Buddhist followers of the Dalai Lama, or Ismaili Shii followers of the Aga Khan or some Ithnashari Shiis loyal to the late Ayatollah Khomeini. Loyalism directed towards an institution or person, however, even if carried to the point of fanaticism, stands in marked contrast to the forms that fundamentalism takes in the scripturally oriented versions of Judaism, Christianity, and Islam, where adherence to the text (or, rather, particular interpretations of the text) supersedes 'traditional' forms of authority. This is especially the case in Arab Muslim societies such as Egypt and Algeria, where the Islamist movements are mostly led, not by members of the religious establishment represented by the traditionally educated rabbical class of *ulama* (learned men) but by religious autodidacts emerging from secondary schools and universities. The revolt of this newly enfranchised class of intellectuals, who usually come from rural backgrounds, has parallels with the Reformation in Europe, which coincided with the invention of printing and the extension of literacy into new social strata. Similarly the original fundamentalists who waged 'battle royal' against the liberals within their own churches to the point where many major Protestant denominations (including Lutherans, Methodists, and Baptists) split into rival synods or churches, were in many cases rebels within their own institutions. Catholic integralists are constrained against rebelling by their loyalty to the leadership.

Inevitably the strains are strongest when the leadership

heresy. The integralists held sway until the 1960s and were crucial in engaging the Church's support for reactionary and fascist movements. Benigni supported Mussolini because he thought that fascism would open the way for the establishment of 'a real party of Christian order which would usher in the final redemption of society' by hastening the demise of a political system into which the Church did not fit.[16] Rather than adjusting the Church's message to the presuppositions of 'scientific criticism' and to conform to the demands of modernity, integralists demand that the Church should act 'as a church for the church'. Hence 'there is no need for Catholicism to become democratic. It is rather the Christian Democracy that should become Catholic.'[17] Wedded to an authoritarian vision of the Catholic Church's organization and mission in the world, integralists lent ideological support to several authoritarian or fascist regimes, such as that of Getulio Vargas in Brazil, Juan Perón in Argentina, General Franco and Opus Dei in Spain, Marshal Pétain and the *Action Française* in France, and Salazar in Portugal.[18] More recent integralist movements include Communion and Liberation in Italy, which sees itself as the one true Church (whose members originally refused to attend Mass with other Catholics) and the Confrontatie group in Holland which monitors other Catholics for signs of heresy. In the United States there are at least two journals, the *Remnant* and the *Wanderer*, which promote integralist views. An article in the *Wanderer*, cited by Coleman, praises two men serving sentences for the bombing one Christmas of three abortion clinics in Florida for giving 'three priceless birthday presents to Jesus'.[19]

The political similarities between integralism and Protestant fundamentalism are compelling, with Vatican support for fascist or proto-fascist regimes matched by fundamentalist support for military dictators such as the 'born-again' Protestant convert Rios Montt, who annihilated whole villages and families in the course of his anti-communist crusade in Guatamala during the 1980s. Montt's reign of terror was probably more influential in converting the Guatamala peasantry to Protestantism than the evangelical views he shared with one of his most ardent supporters the Reverend Pat Robertson. 'The terrifying reality of the displaced Indians more or less matched the worldview offered by fundamentalist evangelicals. Impending doom and the Second Coming of Christ offered both an explanation for their devastated society and a promise of a new and better world in heaven.'[20] There are also religious similarities. The doctrine of papal infallibility adopted at Vatican I (1869–70) was a response to the same liberal or modernizing tendencies to which the original fundamentalists were responding during the first two decades of the twentieth century, with papal infallibility corresponding to biblical inerrancy. In both cases the fundamentalist/integralists 'took central orthodox symbols and blew them out of proportion to form a caricature'[21] while enabling them to appeal to larger constituencies within their respective traditions. Both groups are caught up in a 'battle royal' against their more liberal co-religionists. Both seek to adopt elements of modernity on their own terms, seeking to be *in* modernity (and to influence its direction), but not *of* it.[22]

The differences, however, are also significant. Because integralists are constrained by their orthodoxy to be 'papal legitimists', with the notable exception of Archbishop Lefebvre's group of Catholics who refused to recognize popes after Pius XII, they are reliant on Vatican bureaucrats to promote their cause. When the Church's policy changed in a liberal direction under the sway of non-integralist Vatican officials—for example, when Pius XII encouraged modern biblical scholarship, or after the reforms of Vatican II—the surviving integralists were forced to toe the 'party line', resorting to 'tortured rhetoric' in order to claim that they represented the authentic spirit and letter of the papal reforms.[23]

Just as the Catholic Church only adopted the doctrine of papal infallibility when liberal theology was beginning to make itself felt, the doctrine of scriptural inerrancy only came to the fore among Protestants when traditional understandings of scripture began to be challenged. Before Higher Criticism made inroads into the consciousness of ordinary Protestants during the nineteenth century, the truth of the Bible was simply a given that did not require special defence or even close scrutiny, especially in Protestant America. But from the 1880s pastors fresh from divinity schools with modernist teachers began to absorb Darwinism and Higher Criticism, casting doubt on the historicity of the Old Testament and the miracles recounted in the New.

As explained above, inerrancy is not the same as literalism, and may even produce opposite conclusions. Where literalist readings may logically lead to the 'deconstruction' of texts, inerrancy when pursued systematically requires textual harmonization. Since the inerrant Bible as understood by fundamentalists is supposed to correspond to the historical actuality of real events in real time (as distinct from mythical events whose significance may be understood symbolically or spiritually) conservative commentators try to edit different versions of the same stories into a coherent narrative structure.

A well-known example concerns the New Testament story of the cleansing of the Temple by Jesus, when he threw out the money-lenders. In the synoptic Gospels (Matthew, Mark, and Luke) the incident occurs at the very end of his ministry, at the beginning of Passion week (the week of the Crucifixion); whereas John has it at the very beginning of his ministry. Liberal theologians may explain the discrepancy by showing how John uses the episode to illustrate the essentially Gnostic theme of the Word made Flesh that resonates throughout the fourth Gospel. The conservative commentator Graham Swift provides a much simpler explanation: Jesus cleansed the Temple twice. The same methodology produces two ascensions of Jesus into heaven, since Luke has this occur on the same day as the resurrection whilst Acts makes it happen forty days later, after Jesus had appeared to the disciples. Multiple ascensions, like dual Temple cleansings, allow both narratives to be taken literally, as real events that happened in real time, 'out there' in the world. To be avoided at all costs is the liberal position that 'there was no certain knowledge of the temporal sequence, or that quite contradictory accounts existed, or that some source represented the events in such and such a way, not because that was the way it happened, but because that was important for the theological message of that particular source'.[24]

For conservative Christians, including fundamentalists, it is important to sustain inerrancy by ironing out narrative inconsistencies, since the Gospels themselves are literary texts that aspire to narrative coherence. Herein lies an important difference between the Bible and the Koran. The holy text of Islam does not take the form of a narrative, nor is its structure chronological. The suras (chapters) are assembled approximately in order of length, with the shortest at the end and the longest (apart from the Opening) at the beginning. The sequence also corresponds, very roughly, to reverse chronological order: as you might find in a collection of letters or legal documents in a box-file, the oldest are at the bottom, the most recent near the top.

The Koran is presented by orthodox Islam as the divinely inspired utterances of the Prophet Muhammad—

or, even more piously, as the very Words that God dictated to him—from the beginning of his prophetic ministry (around 610) until his death in 632. Passages in the Koran that refer to historical events such as the Battle of Badr, Muhammad's first important victory against his pagan enemies in 634, are not self-explanatory. In order to understand the context of such passages and to make sense of many others, later generations of scholars had to refer to the secondary body of literature known as the Hadith. These so-called 'Traditions' are reports of the sayings and actions of the Prophet presumed to have been transmitted orally before being assembled in written collections, six of which are regarded by Muslims in the majority Sunni tradition as canonical. While the Koran is regarded by the vast majority of Muslims as the Word of God unmediated by human authorship, arguments about the authenticity of some individual Hadiths existed long before Western scholars trained in biblical studies began to cast their critical eyes upon the whole corpus.

Higher Critical scholarship of the Koran, using methodologies adapted from biblical criticism, is still in its infancy, and largely confined to scholars working in Western universities. So sensitive is this area for Muslims that 'Ibn Warraq', a Muslim-born writer trained in Arabic who accepts the findings of radical Western scholarship, has felt it necessary to publish his work under a pseudonym. In the post-Rushdie atmosphere of cultural confrontation between Islamic and Western worlds, criticism of

BOX 9

Islam as a religious culture has not confused humanistic learning with the revealed word; accordingly it has been spared—or in any event has avoided—the historical acids that have eroded biblical faith and Christian 'culture' since the sixteenth century. Its methods of exegesis, legal reasoning, and political argumentation look peculiar and retrograde to the Westerner precisely because the Westerner—whether a liberal Anglican or an evangelical Christian—stands on the other shore of a sea that Islam has not chosen to cross. It is small consolation to those who yearn for a restoration of Christian values or biblical religion that Christianity did not mean to cross the sea of faith either, or at least had expected, in embarking on its intellectual journey during the Renaissance, to find God on the other side.

(R. Joseph Hoffmann, Preface to 'Ibn Warraq', *Why I am not a Muslim*)

the Koran demands considerably more caution than criticism of the Bible.

Despite the pressures on Western scholarship, the challenge of subjecting the Koran to Higher Critical methods remains open. As with the Bible, the spotting of apparent anomalies or contradictions in the text can lead to the unravelling of the received understanding of the relationship between the text and the circumstances of its appearance. At a rudimentary level the sceptical reader may ask how a text presumed to have been dictated by God or an angel acting for him contains passages (including the

Opening or *Fatiha*) which are clearly prayers or invocations addressed *to* the Almighty. Indeed, throughout the text there is uncertainty or ambiguity about 'who' is addressing whom. As Richard Bell and Montgomery Watt argue in their scholarly *Introduction to the Quran*, 'The assumption that God is himself the speaker in every passage ... leads to difficulties. Frequently God is referred to in the third person. It is no doubt allowable for a speaker to refer to himself in the third person occasionally, but the extent to which we find the Prophet apparently being addressed and told about God as a third person is unusual. It has, in fact, been made a matter of ridicule that in the Quran God is made to swear by himself.'[25] As with the Bible there are issues about the integrity of the text of the Koran. The early Shia sectarians believed that passages favourable to Ali, whom they believed to have been passed over as Muhammad's rightful successor, were suppressed; whilst the puritanical Kharijis (seceders), who split from the mainstream body of Islam before even the Shia, could not believe that the Sura of Joseph which other scholars have seen as a positive celebration of human sexuality, could rightfully belong in the holy book.

Such views, of course, can be dismissed as reflecting the sectarian concerns of those holding them. More problematic are archaeological difficulties including the orientation of the *qibla* (signalling the direction of prayer) in some of the earliest mosques, which point to Jerusalem rather than Mecca. On the basis of textual, archaeological,

BOX 10

[Michael Cook, Patricia Crone, and Martin Hinds] regard the whole established version of Islamic history down at least to the time of ʿAbd al-Malik (685–705) as a later fabrication, and reconstruct the Arab Conquests and the formation of the Caliphate as a movement of peninsular Arabs who had been inspired by Jewish messianism to try to reclaim the Promised Land. In this interpretation, Islam emerged as an autonomous religion and culture only within the process of a long struggle for identity among the disparate peoples yoked together by the Conquests: Jacobite Syrians, Nestorian Aramaeans in Iraq, Copts, Jews and (finally) Peninsular Arabs.

(R. Stephen Humphreys, *Islamic History, A Framework for Inquiry*)

and non-Islamic sources such as the writings of Christian monks, a revisionist school of historiography based mainly in Britain and Germany has developed the bold hypothesis that rather than arising in Arabia (as the Koranic commentaries and biographies of Muhammad constructed out of the Hadith literature relate) 'Islam' emerged as a new religious tradition out of polemics conducted between different factions of Semitic monotheists *after* the conquest of Palestine and the Fertile Crescent by Arabs from the peninsular.

The revisionists' historiography cannot be expected to leave the Koran untouched. John Wansbrough, architect of the revisionist school, argued that the Koran and the

Hadith emerged out of sectarian controversies between Jewish and Christian monotheists over a long period, and were then 'projected back onto an Arabian point of origin'.[26] A follower of this tendency, Gerald Hawting, draws on wide reading in the history of religions to suggest that Muhammad's attacks on polytheists, which are supposed to have occurred in Mecca, actually arose much later in the course of religious polemics between different groups of monotheists in the Levant. As a religious system, writes Hawting, 'Islam, should be understood as the result of an intra-monotheist polemic, in a process similar to that of the emergence of the other main divisions of monotheism'.[27]

Is a belief in the inerrancy of scripture a precondition of 'fundamentalism', a defining characteristic in all traditions? While it may be true that all Christian fundamentalists are inerrantists, the converse does not apply. Many Christian evangelicals who are not fundamentalists believe the Bible to be inerrant; while since the vast majority of believing Muslims are Koranic inerrantists, Islamic fundamentalism cannot really be defined in terms of Koranic inerrancy: if every mainstream believer is described as a 'fundamentalist' then the term ceases to be meaningful.

Since all fundamentalists in the Western monotheist traditions, Christianity, Islam, and (with some reservations) Judaism, may be considered textual inerrantists, a more limited or precise definition is needed if the Islamic radicals are to be included. The key is to be found neither in literalism (which as we have seen is highly problematic) nor in inerrancy (much too broad) but in a common hermeneutic style. Christian and Muslim fundamentalists, and to a lesser degree their Jewish counterparts, share a religious outlook which, paradoxically, has many common features with the secularism or 'materialism' they claim so adamantly to oppose. Rather than calling it 'literalist', I would prefer to describe this style as 'factualist' or historicist.

In her discussion about fundamentalism in *The Battle for God*, Karen Armstrong explains the prevalence of fundamentalism in the three major Western religious traditions by suggesting that two sources of knowledge that were kept apart in pre-modern times, *mythos* and *logos*, the respective preserves of 'timelessness and constancy', have collapsed under the influence of modern religious ideologues, many of whom are trained in the 'hard' or applied sciences. They read religious texts as blueprints for practical action. In pre-modern times, according to Armstrong, people 'evolved two ways of thinking, speaking and acquiring knowledge, which scholars have called *mythos* and *logos*. Both were essential; they were regarded as complementary ways of arriving at truth, and each had its separate area of competence.'[28] Instead of maintaining complementarity, modern religious ideologues have assimilated *mythos* to *logos*, rationalizing and secularizing, as it were, ideas that pre-moderns had safely kept confined to the realm of myth. Thus Armstrong condemns Abd al-Salaam Farrag, the engineer who planned the assassination of Egyptian President Anwar Sadat in 1981 for reading 'the words of scripture as though they were factually true in every detail ... [which] showed yet another danger of using the *mythos* of scripture as a blueprint for practical action. The old ideal had been to keep *mythos* and *logos* separate: political action was the preserve of reason.'[29]

The implication of Armstrong's analysis is that people in pre-modern societies were somehow less prone to take action on the basis of 'mythical' ideas than in modern societies, while begging the question of what constitutes the 'modern'. Her argument flies in the face of historical evidence that many pre-moderns (howsoever defined) enacted their myths in rational terms: the early conquests of Islam and the development of Islamic law, not to mention several eschatologically oriented movements throughout Islamic history, or similar movements in the history of Christianity and Judaism, furnish numerous examples.

A more fruitful approach to modern fundamentalisms would focus on the empowering dimensions of myths as self-validating expressions of the sacred in a pluralistic world in which real power and authority have become diffused and anonymous. As the sociologist Anthony Giddens reminds us, modernity is not so much charac-terized by faith in 'science' (which the philosopher Karl

Popper pointed out, always rests on shifting sands) but on trust in such anonymous abstract systems as the banking system or the depersonalized interactions between engineers, mechanics, pilots, and air traffic controllers that keep passenger jets flying. Trust in abstract systems provides for the reliability of day-to-day living, but by its very nature cannot supply either the mutuality or intimacy offered by relations of personal trust.[30] The latter, as Giddens points out, can only be established through a process of self-enquiry since trust between individuals is based on 'mutual self-disclosure'. The 'discovery of oneself' becomes a project directly involved with the reflexivity of modernity. Hence in the United States Buddhism, Sufism, and other religious traditions centred on 'discovery of the inner self' have become popular religious options.[31]

Although on the face of it fundamentalist movements, with their highly authoritarian appearance, seem to run counter to this trend, closer inspection suggests there may be more similarity between modern 'fundamentalisms' and New Age cults or new religious movements than many observers suppose. Both provide sources of authority in a global environment where actual power is diffused and impersonal. Both can provide psychological reassurance in a world in which areas of relative security interlace with radical doubt and with disquieting scenarios of risk.[32] Not all fundamentalist movements are political. Fundamentalist engagement in politics usually has local causes, not the least of which is the pursuit of power or influence by groups which consider themselves to have been disenfranchised politically or culturally.

While I would question Armstrong's assumption that pre-moderns always kept *mythos* and *logos* in balance, her point about the literalism, or rather the 'factualism', with which modern religious ideologues treat scripture, as manuals for practical action as distinct from sources of personal inspiration or moral guidance, is well made. Research reveals that the majority of Islamist activists, including the civil engineer Osama bin Laden and the architect Mohamed Atta, are drawn not from people trained in theology or religious studies, but from the ranks of graduates in modern faculties such as medicine or engineering who combine a sophisticated knowledge of the technical products of modernity with two-dimensional understandings of their inherited faith tradition. The way in which fundamentalists in all traditions are adept at using modern information technologies, including computer data-systems, audio and video—not to mention that nightmare shared by George Bush and Tony Blair, the possession by religious terrorists of 'weapons of mass destruction' (WMD)—will be considered in a later chapter. Here it would be worth exploring further the problematic relationship between *mythos* and *logos*.

In the widest sense all thought tends towards the mythical because of the way in which the human mind works. The mind is not a computer which dishes up individual words or factoids from a vast electronic memory, performing in seconds calculations that would have taken Einstein a lifetime or more. The mind works by drawing inferences from the data presented to it—by jumping, as it were, to conclusions—on the basis of very limited information. 'A description of our minds as a bundle of inference systems, differently activated by different objects, is better than that of a mental encyclopedia because it is much closer to the way a brain is actually organised' writes Pascal Boyer in *Religion Explained*, a book which combines an anthropological approach to religion with recent discoveries in cognitive science and evolutionary biology.[33]

Myths, like poetry, exploit our inference systems. They encapsulate thought rather than teasing or spelling it out logically. The philosopher Karl Jaspers saw myth as the 'first order of knowing'. Contrary to Auguste Comte, the philosopher of positivism, and Rudolf Bultmann, the theologian who believed that Christianity must be 'demythologized', Jaspers argued the case for myth as a source of creative power, a 'seedbed of metaphor, symbolism and ideas out of which later reflection and analysis have developed'.[34] The great exemplars for using myth as a 'seedbed of symbolism' were Sigmund Freud and C. G. Jung. Freud found in the myth of Oedipus a way of encapsulating the paradoxes and complexities of human sexuality; Jung deployed myth as a means of exploring the archaeology of consciousness through the surfacing of religious symbols and archetypes in dreams.

Fundamentalists of course utterly reject Comte's belief

that religious myths would be replaced by scientific positivism as a way of explaining the world; while Bultmann's 'demythologized Christianity' has long been one of their principal targets. Arguably by demythologizing Christianity Bultmann was actually 're-mythologizing' it, since by interpreting it symbolically and existentially he deprived it of its historical factuality. For his Christian critics, who are not just conservatives or fundamentalists, Bultmann's interpretation of the Christian story leaves no room for a historical revelation in time.

Formally speaking, fundamentalists utterly reject the 'subjectivization' of religion or its internalization into the private recesses of the self. A century before Jung, William Blake anticipated the Swiss psychoanalyst by insisting that 'all deities reside in the human breast'. 'Jesus was the Son of God,' proclaimed Blake, 'but so am I, and so are you ...'.35 Yet Blake's mystical religiosity was not far removed from that of those born-again Christians who follow the moderate Southern Baptist theologian E. Y. Mullins in describing the conversion experience as 'falling in love with Jesus'. American fundamentalists do not reject the subjective, mythical 'Jesus of the heart' in their rebellion against modernism. Indeed those millions of 'born-again Christians' who claim to have taken Jesus as their 'personal' saviour are closer to Blake's heretical Gnosticism than most of them would acknowledge. But they also demand the restoration of the historical Jesus along with an inerrant Bible that is true 'in all realms of reality' and 'all fields of knowledge'—as the Statement on Scripture passed by the Southern Baptist Convention following the fundamentalist victory in 1987 has it.[36] The imagination, which Blake described as the 'Divine Body in Every Man', is fed and fructified by myth. But for fundamentalists, who take myth in its popular sense of 'lie', as distinct from an archetypical or elemental truth, myth must be collapsed into history—the record of things as they actually happened in the world of verifiable, external reality. And since the Bible contains a number of prophetic books, a literal or factualistic reading of it describes events that will occur in the foreseeable historical future.

The collapsing of myth into history is one of the most prominent of the 'family resemblances' by which different members of the fundamentalist tribe may be identified. Though prominent among premillennial Protestants, it is far from being confined to them. Sayyid Qutb, the Islamist ideologue, though a man of great literary sensitivity, urged his followers to approach the Koran as a manual for action, as distinct from a source of moral or spiritual guidance. The first generation of Muslims, he argued, did not approach the Koran for the purpose of acquiring culture and information, nor for taste or enjoyment. None of them came to it simply for the sake of knowledge itself, to solve scientific or legal problems or to remove some defect in his understanding. Rather he turned to the Koran 'to find out what the Almighty Creator had prescribed for him and for the group in which he lived, for his life and for the life of the group'. He approached it in order to act upon it immediately, 'as a soldier on the battlefield reads his daily bulletin so that he knows what is to be done'.[37] For Qutb and his disciples the 'Sword' verses in the Koran urging Holy War against the enemies of God are to be interpreted currently as operational manuals, rather than as broader spiritual guidance against the forces of evil. Qutb is the intellectual who shaped the thinking of Osama bin Laden and most of today's Islamist groups.

A similar collapsing of foundational myth into contemporary action informs Jewish extremism. In the Bible[38] the Children of Israel are commanded by God to massacre the Amalekites, an indigenous Caananite tribe, along with their women, children, and flocks. For fundamentalist militants such as Rabbi Yisrael Hess, formerly the campus rabbi of Tel Aviv's Bar-Ilan University, the Amalekites of scripture are assimilated to contemporary Palestinian Arabs: an article by the rabbi entitled 'The Commandment of Genocide in the Torah', cited in a book by Yehoshafat Harkabi, a former director of Israeli military intelligence, ends with the chilling words: 'The day will yet come when we will all be called to fulfil the commandment of the divinely ordained war to destroy Amalek.'[39]

Biblical eschatology collapses past and future, putting history into reverse. For many American fundamentalists the return of Christ will be preceded by the war against the Antichrist and the Days of Tribulation, when those who have not been saved will perish miserably in a series of catastrophic disasters. A popular version of the apocalyptic events predicted in the Book of Revelation, Hal Lindsay's *Late Great Planet Earth*, first published in 1970, has sold more than 30 million copies to date.

A small, but critical, step separates such predictions from their concretization or enactment. Most fundamentalists are content to let the divine will take its course, unaided by human intervention. But when the divine is actualized and brought onto the plane of history, humans inevitably become its self-appointed instruments. In Israel there have been several attempts by Jewish fundamentalists to destroy the Dome of the Rock and al-Aqsa Mosque which were built on the site of the Second Temple destroyed by the Romans in 66 CE. At his trial on terrorist charges one of the plotters, Yehuda Etzion, challenged the competence of the Israeli court to sit in judgement over him: God had given him personal responsibility to advance the process of redemption through radical action.[40] There is a registered association, the Faithful of Temple Mount, which demands that the Dome be levelled and the site purified by the slaughter of a pure white heifer, as prescribed in the Bible, before the new temple is built. As pure white heifers are extremely rare, the association is funding a breeding programme in the United States with the aim of producing such an animal.

Messianic movements built around eschatological expectations are a constant of human history and potent engines of change. The future goal of a classless society to which the founders of modern communism aspired was rooted in a secularized version of Judaeo-Christian eschatology. There are close parallels in the Nazi idea of a Thousand Year Reich. That history progresses teleologically towards a final eschatological denouement is fundamental to the Judaeo-Christian outlook. As several historians including Christopher Hill and Norman Cohn have shown, revolutionary movements in pre-modern times such as the Fifth Monarchy Men of the English Revolution or the Anabaptists of Münster were fuelled by chiliastic expectations and end of the world scenarios. The hope for a communist utopia drew deeply on these age-old utopian hopes. For Marxism and fascism, however, there was a crucial difference: the lack of a supernatural agency to bring about the doomsday scenario. As Leszek Kolakowsky, one of the most perceptive critics of Marxism, explained at a time when he still considered himself a Marxist, 'This secular eschatology, this belief in the future elimination of the disparity between man's essence and his existence presupposes, obviously, that "essence" is a value, that its realisation is desirable, and that the wisdom of history will bring about its realisation. Secular eschatology trusts the final judgement of history.'[41]

The difference, however, between an eschatology predicated on supernatural intervention and one founded on human action may be slighter than one might think, for fundamentalist action involves, almost by definition, the appropriation of the divine will. As a 'Defender of God' the fundamentalist militant claims the right to act on his behalf. By collapsing myth into history, by taking action for God, fundamentalism paradoxically affirms the supremacy of the human will, unwittingly following the madman in Nietzsche's story who proclaimed the Death of God.*

* In Nietzsche's parable in *The Gay Science* (1882), a madman runs into the market place crying 'I seek God! I seek God!' When the bystanders ask him where he imagines God has gone, the madman glares at them furiously. 'Where has God gone? . . . I mean to tell you. We have killed him, you and I! We are all his murderers!'

Although the ritual burning of widows became illegal throughout India after the British governor of Bengal, Lord Bentinck, banned it in 1829, the practice has acquired iconic status as an 'act of spiritual sacrifice' and like similar practices, such as dowry murders, female infanticide, and, latterly, the abortion of females when the sex of a foetus has been determined by amniocentesis, has proved difficult to eradicate. Thirty-seven people, three of them minors, were accused of abetting Roop Kanwar's illegal immolation, including the bride's father-in-law and her brother, who lit the pyre. None of the indictments was successful because no one who attended the ceremony was prepared to risk prosecution under the Sati (Prevention of Glorification) Act by giving evidence in court. Within a year Roop Kanwar's shrine was attracting thousands of visitors. The money collected from voluntary donations amounted to more than 70 lakh rupees (more than $250 thousand), an immense sum in one of India's poorest districts. Despite laws enacted with the specific purpose of banning pro-*sati* propaganda in local and national elections, 4,000 visitors attended the anniversary of Roop Kanwar's *sati* in 1988. When the authorities stopped public transport from Deorala, the pilgrims arrived on foot, by camel cart or private buses, crowded with people on their roofs or hanging from the windows. More than 800 wayside booths appeared, selling souvenirs, snacks, toys, coconuts and incense—along with the inevitable photo collages of the smiling Roop and her husband enveloped by flames.[1]

Fundamentalism or tradition? Murder or suicide? The ultimate symbol of female oppression or an ironic, if extreme, demonstration of a 'woman's right to choose'? The questions raised by the *sati* of Roop Kanwar are not just significant in themselves: they concern our discussion of the 'F-word'—its semantic biography as it were—because the Deorala bride's immolation seems to have been the occasion for its introduction into the lexicon of Indian English. According to John Stratton Hawley, 'fundamentalism' began to be widely used in the context of the Hindu revival in India in the reports of the Deorala *sati*, which filled the newspapers for many months. Since then, 'in Indian newspapers and periodicals, the word *fundamentalism* has gradually phased out such terms as *revivalism* and *obscurantism*', reflecting more closely 'the British ambience that has dominated English-language education in India' and the outlook of India's secular-minded, English-speaking elites.

For its supporters, who included the weighty figure of Shankayracharya of Puri, one of the four 'pontiffs' or heads of the Advaita religious tradition, *sati* is a profoundly spiritual act by which a woman achieves immortality for herself and her husband. By remaining at his side during the cremation, she shelters him from the spiritual dangers of death, cancelling any karmic shortcomings accrued during his lifetime, as well as offering benefits to those who witness her act. Like the suicide martyrs in Chechnya and Israel-Palestine, the *sati*'s family derives spiritual

BOX 11

If the woman pursues her desire to become sati from motives of genuine devolution to her husband, the truth of her stance is believed to become plain at the moment she dies. As she enters the world beyond this life, her divinity becomes manifest in this one: with no physical assistance from the outside, the fire of her inner truth (sat) ignites her pyre. People seek out such a sati in the hours prior to this happening, for although her divinity is concealed from public view, it is present nonetheless ... Once her sat bursts forth in flames, she becomes a 'sati mother' (*satimata*) fully capable of nurturing and sheltering her 'children' well into future generations. She joins other 'sati mothers' in a class so tightly-knit that her worshippers are apt to refer to any member of it as if she were the whole. She is thus in some sense the goddess Sati—a member of a sacred class to which the wife of Shiva called Sati also belongs.

(John Stratton Hawley, *Fundamentalism and Gender*)

benefit from her act of sacrifice: the blessings she accrues are enjoyed by seven generations before and after her.

For its detractors, who include the Shankayracharya of Kanchipuram, *sati* is far from being a necessary part of Hindu tradition. According to this authority the philosopher, seer, and teacher Adi Shankara, from whom all the Shankayracharyas derive their spiritual authority, condemned the practice more than a thousand years before the British intervention. Feminist activists and writers see

BOX 12

> Smothered or poisoned at birth, given away in marriage at a tender age, bargained over like some commodity by dowry-hungry in-laws, secluded in the name of chastity and religion, and finally burned for the exaltation of the family's honour, or shunned as inauspicious widows, the burden of oppression took different forms at different stages of a [Hindu] woman's life, from birth to death, in a chain of attitudes linked by contempt for the female.
>
> (Sakuntala Narasimhan, *Sati: A Study of Widow Burning in India*)

the practice as a ritualized instance of violence against women, as part of the spiritual nexus which enslaves Hindu women psychologically, encouraging abuse by denying their individuality and confining them to the household. For Sakuntala Narasimhan, a journalist and musician, *sati* is merely the most egregious of a raft of degrading practices to which Indian women are constantly subjected.

The use of the 'F-word' is especially problematical when applied to Hinduism, since unlike the Abrahamic traditions of Judaism, Christianity, and Islam, there is no single text, such as the Bible or the Koran, identified with the Word of God or supreme religious authority. The Hindu scriptures consist of a massive body of texts dating back more than four thousand years and added to over the centuries: the example, *par excellence*, of what scholars call 'cumulative tradition'. Claims that there are references to *sati* in the Rig Veda, one of the oldest of the Vedic texts, and the Mahabharata, the most famous of the Hindu epics, have been challenged by scholars who argue that the custom is of much more recent origin. Narasimhan points out that the Baghavad Gita, the section of the Mahabharata that has come to be seen as the supreme statement of Hindu ethics, argues that morality must be disinterested, condemning actions based on the expectation of future rewards: 'hence immolation in the expectation of felicity in an afterlife can only be immoral'.[2] In justification of *sati* the Shankayracharya of Puri cited sixteenth- and seventeenth-century texts that date from the period of turbulence and upheaval following the Moghul conquests. This seems consistent with the scholarly view that *sati* may be an 'invented' patriarchal tradition that originated among the nobility (the Kshatriya class) rather than the priestly class of Brahmins, as a means of ensuring that their women were not violated by invading armies.

The Rajputs of Rajasthan, who take pride in their warrior traditions, encouraged their women to immolate themselves in a rite known as *jauhar* rather than submit to being raped by invaders. In 1295, before the fall of Jaisalmer, 24,000 women are said to have been burned to death; just before the fall of Chittor in 1569, 300 women led by Queen Padmimi committed mass suicide inside the fortress rather than be taken captive and violated by the invading Afghan armies of Ala-ud-din.[3] As Hawley suggests, there is a close connection between *sati* and the memory of *jauhar* in Rajasthan. Sociologically, the defence of *sati* appears to be related to the rise of the Marwawi community, an important group of North Indian merchants whose homeland lies in the area around the town of Jhunjhunu in Rajasthan. The Great Queen Sati temple at Jhunjhunu, not far from Deorala, is the nation's largest and wealthiest *sati* temple, drawing tens of thousands of visitors each year. It commemorates the Rani Sati, a maternal manifestation of the divinity. As the 15-year-old bride of an unconsummated marriage, she was so dedicated to her husband that she chose *sati* rather than life as a widow. The cult of the Rani Sati reinforces the Marwawi clan's group identity, acting as the primary focus of their communal bond. The Jhunjhunu temple has inspired the construction of several *sati* temples in Delhi.[4]

Despite the problematic use of the 'F-word' outside the textually based Abrahamic religious tradition, at least two 'family resemblances' suggest a relationship between the pro-*sati* movement in India and 'fundamentalisms' in other religious traditions. The first—to be looked at more closely in the next chapter—is the 'politicization of religion' and its relationship with nationalism, both cultural and political. The second is the closely related issue of gender. Politically, the Bharatiya Janata Party, which today leads India's governing coalition, was intimately involved in the pro-*sati* cause in Rajasthan, with one of its leaders, Vijayaraje Scindia, insisting that a 'voluntary act of self-immolation by a widow in dedication to her husband' should not be allowed to constitute an offence in law. The head of the Janata party in Rajasthan, Kalyan Singh Kalvi, responded to the criticism that *sati* demeans women by stating: 'In our culture, we worship the motherland, *dharma*, and *nari*', thereby making a direct connection between motherland, religion, and woman.[5] Rather than being seen as the defence of an exotic item of religious heritage threatened with extinction, the pro-*sati* agitation can be seen as part of a counter-feminist or patriarchal protest movement that is common ground among fundamentalists in all traditions.

In a pioneering study that looked in detail at two versions of religious fundamentalism—the original fundamentalism of early twentieth-century America and the Shii Islamic version which came to power in Iran 1979—the sociologist Martin Riesebrodt saw both as aspects of a common 'patriarchal protest movement'. Though he refrained from drawing wider conclusions, there is plenty of evidence to suggest that his approach can be applied to fundamentalisms not just in Iran and America, but in many other places currently being affected by politicized, public religiosity.[6]

Several recent studies suggest that sex—or more specifically, the control of female sexuality—looms large in the language employed by fundamentalists. In the 1920s American fundamentalists like John R. Straton explicitly linked the public expression of female sexuality to the

BOX 13

The wave of animalism which is sweeping over the world today, and the degradation of the modern dance, the sensualism of the modern theatre, the glorification of the flesh in modern styles, and the sex suggestion of modern literature, the substitution of dogs for babies, the appalling divorce evil, have all come about because of this degrading philosophy of animalism which evolution is spreading over the earth.

(J. R. Straton, *Searchlight*, 7/12, Feb. 1924)

corrosive effects of Darwinism—or what he preferred to call, polemically, 'animalism'.

Revolutionary Islamist groups like the Fedayan-i Islam denounce unveiled women in similar, if more dramatic, language: 'Flames of passion rise from the naked bodies of immoral women and burn humanity to ashes', causing young men to neglect their work. More than half the provisions of a 1981 law introduced in the Islamic Republic to codify Koranic prescriptions—107 out of 195 articles—were concerned with sexual activities, ranging from the prosecution of adultery and homosexuality to preventing unrelated persons of the same sex lying naked under a blanket.[7]

Reisebrodt sees the obsessive concern with sexuality common to American and Iranian fundamentalisms as a reaction to broader anxieties resulting from rural displacement and economic change. Fundamentalism is a protest against the assault on patriarchal principles in the family, economy, and politics.[8] The symptoms of patriarchal decline, he argues, manifest themselves primarily in the spheres of the family and sexual morality; but the underlying causes may lie in those very processes the sociologist Max Weber regarded as integral to modernity: the expansion of large-scale 'rationalized' operations, entailing formalized and codified relationships, at the expense of small businesses based on intimate paternalistic relations between employers and employees. In resisting such aspects of what Weber famously called the 'disenchantment of the world', fundamentalisms may appear to be 'anti-modern'. But reality forces them to absorb many of modernity's salient features.

According to Riesebrodt, what fundamentalists cannot prevent in the way of structural transformation they attempt to impose symbolically. A gender-based division of labour is found in nearly all pre-modern societies. Under today's conditions it can no longer be sustained by traditional domestic arrangements, since in most modern societies women are required in the workforce. Instead segregation is achieved by symbolic means such as sartorial coding—long hair and skirts for American women with 'Christian' haircuts (short back and sides) for their menfolk; the veil in its various forms for Muslim women, the beard—a mark of sex and piety—for men. These forms of public religiosity may mask, but do not necessarily reverse or even delay, the processes of secularization.

In assessing the impact of fundamentalisms on women, and families, Helen Hardacre endorses Riesebrodt's perspectives, arguing that family values are so basic to religious thought and behaviour that at times when social or political changes affect the family, religions are liable to react as though they are being undermined at their very foundations. The responses of particular religions may differ widely, but most of them share the perception that values 'traditionally' associated with the family are under threat. 'Many fundamentalist movements ... pursue social programs designed to reshape the family in accord with these values. These programs in turn share another trait: they define the role of women and children quite narrowly and often place severe restrictions on these family members.'[9]

For Hardacre, Islamic fundamentalism is, amongst other things, 'a patriarchal protest movement against selected aspects of secularized modernity'.[10] The same can be said, with modifications, for other fundamentalisms, nearly all of which affirm different roles for men and women, with the latter expected to carry the burden of childcare. However, given the varied social worlds in which fundamentalists actually operate, the results are far from being uniform. Nor are they necessarily reactionary or conservative.

In Latin America, where men often abandon their children, the patriarchal ideology promoted by evangelical churches encourages them to be more responsible fathers.

Women, the 'voiceless' group in the region, 'find in evangelical and Pentecostal communities the space and opportunity to exercise their gifts' while their husbands 'are encouraged to encounter a relational and affective part of themselves denied by the traditional macho culture'.[11] Similarly, Japanese New Religions, some of which were founded by female prophets, theoretically reinforce ideals of male dominance while actually allowing women more active and participatory roles than traditional Buddhism and Shinto. In Sri Lanka, a women's Buddhist movement, the *dasa-sil-mata*, is campaigning to restore a long defunct order of Buddhist nuns, against resistance from several male-dominated Buddhist organizations. Even in Iran, where many female workers were purged after the 1979 revolution, the situation is not unambiguous, as the revolution has encouraged the emergence of middle-class feminists determined to reinterpret Islam as empowering them rather than restricting their activities.

In the Islamic world particularly, the issue has been confused by the symbolism of the veil and its ambiguities. In the twentieth century, women's emancipation in Egypt, Iran, and other Muslim countries was symbolized by the abandoning of the veil by upper-class women under the influence of Western culture, or in some cases its abolition by reforming autocrats. Abolished by decree by unpopular governments, the veil could easily be transformed into an emblem of cultural or political resistance. In Algeria veiled Muslim women played an active part in the struggle for independence against France. In Egypt, as Andrea Rugh suggests, the fundamentalist ideology which insists on veiling for women may actually reflect an emancipation from family bonds, rather than an endorsement of them. Young women who wear the *hijab* ('veil' or religious dress) no longer seek their parent's permission to visit mosques or attend religious meetings. Allah replaces the father as the ultimate authority for individuals, while stressing their obligations to the wider community.[12]

At the same time real horror stories abound. A recent example has been the fate of women in Afghanistan, a landlocked, mountainous country where patriarchal tribal customs have retained their hold for much longer than elsewhere. Among the Ghizlai the women are secluded from non-*mahrams*—men other than fathers or brothers to whom they could be married. Among the Pushtuns, a bride who does not bleed on her wedding night may be killed by her father or brothers. 'Honour killings' for alleged sexual misconduct by women are far from being limited to mountainous, tribal regions: they occur in many other parts of the world, and though Jordan, Egypt, Syria, and Iraq furnish numerous examples, honour killings are far from being confined to Muslim societies. The culture of 'honour and shame' in which masculine honour and identity are predicated on female virtue, is also found in Catholic Spain and Sicily and the Orthodox Balkans.

Among the Afghani Pushtuns, however, the patriarchal structures are as confining to women as any on the planet.

The Pushtunwali—the Pushtun customary law—differs in signal respects from Islamic legal practice elsewhere. Divorce (a possibility in mainstream Islam, though easier for men than women) is prohibited and women are prevented from owning land (contrary to the provisions of normative Islamic law). Women are wholly regarded as the property of men and 'as pawns in economic and political exchanges' with marriages, enforced or otherwise, used as a way to end tribal feuds, to cement alliances between clans, or to increase a family's prestige.[13] According to a well-known Pushtun saying, 'a woman is best either in the household or in the grave', with *purdah* (seclusion and veiling outside the household) regarded as a 'key element in protecting the family's pride and honour'.[14] Because of male resistance, over 90 per cent of Afghan women remained illiterate until recently. (The current rate is still about 80 per cent for women, compared with about 50 per cent for men.)

The political oscillations afflicting Afghanistan since the turn of the twentieth century have revolved very largely around the 'woman question' and the issue of female segregation. From the 1920s governments in Kabul had strongly supported women's education. King Amanullah (1919–29), like his contemporary Reza Shah Pahlevi in Iran, urged women to come out of *purdah*. Heeding his advice, members of the Westernized elite took to wearing European clothes, with skirts to the knee and heads uncovered. When Amanullah was overthrown by conservative tribesmen in 1929, women were put back in *purdah* and forced to wear the *chadari* or *burqa*, the tent-like garment that covers the whole body, leaving only a small grille for the eyes. *Purdah* remained in force until 1959 when Prime Minister Daoud Khan announced the voluntary end of seclusion and removal of the veil. In the 1960s miniskirts began to appear in the capital and unveiled female television announcers became stars for the minority of (mainly urban) people with television sets. Nevertheless unveiled, educated women encountered brutal opposition, with women wearing Western dress, including teachers and schoolgirls, having their exposed legs shot at or splashed with acid. Generally, the pattern was far from uniform, with considerable variation between cities such as ultraconservative Kandahar and more liberal Herat and Kabul.

In April 1978 the People's Democratic Party of Afghanistan (PDPA) seized power in a *coup d'état*. The new socialist government, which included a number of women at senior level, immediately enacted changes in family law to improve the status of women while encouraging female education and employment. Massive spending on weddings, a major cause of poverty, was discouraged. A decree on marriage limited the size of dowries and forbade the exchange of women for cash or kind. Literacy classes, including compulsory classes for women, were established in rural areas. Inspired by socialist ideals and the considerable advances in education and women's emancipation that had taken place in the neighbouring Soviet republics of Central Asia, the new rulers of Afghanistan adopted a radical modernist outlook, one 'which linked Afghan backwardness to feudalism, widespread female illiteracy and the exchange of girls'.[15]

All these measures encountered massive resistance from conservative tribal forces. In Kandahar female literacy workers were murdered. On at least two occasions the men killed all the women in their families to prevent them from 'dishonouring' them. The new marriage rules enraged rural landowners, who regarded women as a form of currency in property exchanges. Compulsory education for girls raised the prospect that they might stop submitting to family (i.e. male) authority. The Soviet invasion in 1979, intended to prop up the faction-ridden socialist government, sparked a vigorous and ultimately successful national resistance movement, backed by Saudi Arabia, Pakistan, and (clandestinely) the United States. In what would become a global *jihad* (struggle or 'holy war') against the Soviet occupation, women were notably absent. Unlike most anti-colonial movements (including the Algerian struggle against France) Afghan women played virtually no part in the *jihad*. They were, however, conspicuous on the pro-Soviet side, with four out of seven militia commanders appointed to the communist Revolutionary Council being women.

When the ultra-conservative Taliban took over in 1996, after several years of civil strife and tribal conflict that followed the Soviet withdrawal in 1989, Afghanistan's

BOX 14

Let us state what sort of education the UN wants. This is a big infidel policy which gives such obscene freedom to women, which would lead to adultery and herald the destruction of Islam. In any Islamic country where adultery becomes common, that country is destroyed and enters the domination of the infidels because their men become like women and women cannot defend themselves. Anybody who talks to us should do so within Islam's framework. The Holy Koran cannot adjust itself to other people's requirements. People should adjust themselves to the requirements of the Holy Koran.

(Maulvi Jalilullah Maulvizada, interviewed by Ahmed Rashid, June 1997)

gender war reached its nadir. Within three months of the capture of Kabul the Taliban closed 63 schools in the Afghan capital, depriving more than 100,000 girls of education along with 150,000 boys. They shut down Kabul University, sending home 10,000 students, of whom 4,000 were women. Female employees were stripped of their jobs, creating chaos in public health and social services. As many as 150,000 women may have been affected by the prohibitions on women's employment, including teachers, doctors, nurses, and civil servants. Sophisticated, educated urban women were forced to wear the *burqa*: decrees passed by the Taliban even banned the Iranian-style headscarf, or *hijab*, as an unacceptable foreign fashion imports.

The Taliban regime, which ended in October 2001, following America's aerial bombardment, is the most extreme example of a misogynistic, reactionary trend that is to be found throughout the developing world, especially in South Asia and the Middle East. But it is also strong in other countries where conservative versions of Islam hold sway. Although female education is encouraged by the state, Saudi women are still forbidden to drive motor vehicles (obliging them, ironically, to rely on the services of chauffeurs or taxi drivers to whom they are not related by blood or marriage). In a notorious episode that made international headlines in 2001 fifteen girls at a boarding school in Jedda were burned to death when their dormitory caught fire. The religious police closed the gates on them because they had not covered themselves according to the requirements of 'strict female modesty' prevailing in the desert kingdom. As in some other Gulf states, Saudi women are not allowed to travel abroad unless accompanied by male relatives. Even in comparatively liberal Sudan, where the National Islamic Front prides itself on its activist female cadres, a woman must have her brother or husband's permission when applying for a passport. In Pakistan, the Hudood (punishment) ordinances passed by the military ruler General Zia al-Haqq, under fundamentalist pressure, effectively equated rape with adultery (*zina*), a crime which, though punishable by death in Islamic law, requires four independent adult male witnesses for its prosecution. The effect of this law has been to make it virtually impossible for a women to press charges against rapists without themselves incurring accusations of adultery. Even in the United States where women have more autonomy and sexual freedom than in most other countries, sixteen states have failed to repeal laws restricting abortion under Christian fundamentalist pressures following the Supreme Court's landmark ruling in *Roe* v. *Wade* (1973).

This catalogue of atrocities and indignities inflicted on women and the restrictions on their freedom imposed on them in many parts of the world would generally seem to support the claims of Riesebrodt, Hardacre, and others that 'fundamentalisms' may indeed be 'patriarchal protest movements', responses by religious conservatives in all traditions to social changes, particularly those affecting the status of women, imposed by governments such as the PDPA in Afghanistan, the result of legal rulings, such as the *Roe* v. *Wade* decision legalizing abortion in the United States, or access to jobs and public spaces previously reserved for men made possible by the logic of economic change. Such responses, however, are very far from being uniform in their effects. It would be wrong to see fundamentalist 'ideology' as being invariably reactionary, not least because women are among its principal supporters.

What prompts women to sign up to religious movements that many would see as inimical to their interests? While generalizations are problematic, it is a fair assumption that nearly all fundamentalist groups or churches studied by scholars reject legal steps to ensure equality between the sexes and typically exclude women from the senior ranks of religious leadership.[16] All—or almost all—express concern about control of female sexuality.[17] All draw strict boundaries between male and female realms. All are hostile to homosexuality, transvestism, and other behaviours that transgress these boundaries. All profess to admire the 'chaste' or 'virtuous' woman while deriding the so-called 'free' or 'secular' woman, whether the latter is seen as a manifestation of the godless hedonism of popular culture, or the product of alien 'Western' lifestyles perceived as threatening to national identity.

It may be argued, of course, that all the major religions are fundamentally patriarchal since they came into being at historical periods distant from our own when human survival was predicated on a strict division of male and female realms. As the hero Arjuna tells the God Krishna in the *Baghavad Gita,*

> 'In overwhelming chaos, Krishna
> Women of the family are corrupted,
> And when women are corrupted,
> Disorder is born in society'[18]

In the languages of Islam the word *fitna*, strife, is applied both to the early dissentions and civil wars that afflicted the primitive Islamic community after the death of the Prophet Muhammad, and the social strife that is seen to be the inevitable consequence of female unchastity. Orthodox Judaism preserves ancient taboos on menstruation, while women are seen as inferior to the extent that they are exempted from the primary religious duty of studying the Torah and Halakha. In the Genesis story, common to Judaism and Christianity, it is Eve, the weaker moral vessel, who is created from Adam's rib and who, beguiled by the serpent, tempts Adam to sin. St Augustine, the most influential of the early church fathers, irons out the contradictions in Genesis and Paul to make the case for female inferiority.[19] Feminist theologians in all the Abrahamic traditions have found ways of rereading the scriptures in order to demonstrate that the original texts are less misogynistic than they appear, that androcentric readings are false or narrowly partisan, and that alternative feminist readings have equal validity. Such efforts, how-ever, while enabling women believers to participate more fully in religious activities previously reserved for men, are not in themselves sufficient to explain the appeal that fundamentalist versions of religion have for women.

In the first place one should not underestimate the attraction that charismatic, male preachers have for female followers. In the Pentecostal tradition preachers such as Jimmy Swaggart (before his fall from grace after a much publicized encounter with a prostitute) project a powerful image of masculinity in line with the macho, militant Christianity proclaimed by Billy Sunday early in the twentieth century. A more measured and sober figure like Jerry

BOX 15

Jesus Christ intended his church to be militant as well as persuasive. It must fight as well as pray ... The prophets all carried the Big Stick ... Strong men resist, weaklings compromise ... Lord save us from off-handed, flabby-cheeked, brittle-boned, weak-kneed, thin-skinned, pliable, plastic, spineless, effeminate, sissified, three-caret Christianity.

(Billy Sunday, *Evening Times* (Trenton, NJ), 6 Jan. 1916)

Falwell may appeal to female followers for his fatherly appearance. Television encourages this, for while God the Father cannot be seen on camera, mature and pleasant-looking men who speak on his behalf such as Falwell and Pat Robertson may provide iconically satisfying substitutes. Authoritative Muslim divines, such as Sheikh Yousuf al-Qaradawi, who has a regular slot on the al-Jazeera TV channel based in Qatar, are immensely popular with female viewers; while Osama bin Laden, vilified by the West as the leader of the al-Qaeda terrorist organization, has carefully made himself into an icon, modelled on the Prophet Muhammad—an image that may exercise a powerful appeal to Muslim women.

But there are also more practical, down-to-earth reasons why women may be drawn to fundamentalist movements. Part of the appeal, as Hardacre suggests, may be economic: in America, for example, although most women can support themselves by their own labour, most of the jobs available to women are less well paid than men's, suggesting that even in an advanced industrial society women may 'live at a higher level when solely supported by a male'.[20] Fundamentalist emphasis on 'family values' with women seen primarily in their capacity as mothers, wives, and homemakers is 'perceived as having an element of economic realism, that is, legitimating and sanctifying an economic inevitability'.[21] In the developing world economic realism may be reinforced by cultural nationalism and anti-colonial sentiment. In Islamic countries the *hijab* in its various guises proclaims a symbolic rejection of Western cultural and economic power (while affording a tacit acceptance of its benefits). Here the dislocating effects of industrialization and rapid urbanization affect men and women equally. While 'the general message of a return to "tradition" as the key to the ills of dislocation and disempowerment is as readily accepted by women as by men'[22] in Islamic countries, the veil, as an invented or reinvented tradition, accommodates changing economic realities by enabling women to work without inviting the unwelcome attentions of men. Where veiling is compulsory, as in post-revolutionary Iran, fundamentalist readings of the legal texts may serve to 'commoditize' and 'fetishize' women by focusing obsessively on their sexuality and reproductive potential.[23] Where it is espoused voluntarily, as among many young Muslims living in Western countries, the message it conveys may be the exact opposite. By concealing her body from the stranger's gaze, the wearer proclaims that she is not a sexual object to be judged by her physical appearance.

In a confused, and confusing world in which gender roles are changing or under constant review, the sexual bipolarity encouraged by fundamentalists everywhere may be reassuring. Fundamentalism addresses the competing claims of children and career by seeming to authenticate motherhood, giving it priority over the feminist goal of human self-development; its values offer women a vision of financial and social security, provided they toe the line drawn by male religious leaders. The religious activities fostered by fundamentalism may facilitate female networking, providing fundamentalist women with the kind of gender solidarity or sisterly support to be found, for example, in feminist group activities. In Western countries the encouragement of 'family values'—along with church-based charitable activities—by conservative politicians lightens the burden of welfare carried by the taxpaying citizen, thereby restricting (in rhetoric, if not always in reality) the reach of the state over civil society. In the Americas especially, fundamentalism as well as some versions of non-fundamentalist evangelicalism, such as Robert Schuller's 'theology of self-esteem', acts as a 'liberation theology of the right', lending a sense of empowerment to people who had previously felt themselves to be marginalized in a culture addicted to hedonistic self-gratification and sexual profanity.

It would be wrong to underestimate the appeal of fundamentalism for women in societies where issues such as teenage pregnancy, AIDS, and drug abuse are matters of public concern. In 'old' Europe such issues are primarily regarded as the concern of local or national government. In laissez-faire America where the state is less committed to social spending and less inclined to intervene in the operation of market forces, old-fashioned Puritan virtue, rooted in America's founding mythology, retains a powerful popular appeal. Prosperity theology, implicit in the images of comfortable, middle-class Christians that appear on popular television shows such as Pat Robertson's *700 Club* or Robert Schuller's *Hour of Power* becomes explicit when television preachers finance their ministries by direct appeals for funds. The telethons to which viewers of 'Christian' programming are regularly exposed show heart-warming stories of people who pledge their 15 dollars a month for Jesus, despite desperate financial circumstances. They are rewarded, not just in heaven, but in their earthly bank accounts: previously sluggish investments suddenly yield handsome dividends, the unemployed 'partner in Christ' lands a well-paid job. Reversing centuries of Christian teachings on poverty, prosperity theology reveals the secular, this-worldly heaven in store for born-again Christians. As the economically more vulnerable section of society, women may be especially susceptible to a message that promises tangible rewards for virtue and abstinence.

Similar considerations, modified to suit different cultural conditions, apply in the Islamic world, where the welfare organizations run by Islamist or fundamentalist movements such as the Gamaat al-Islamiya in Egypt or Hamas in Palestine are often better equipped to address the needs of desperately needy people than the corrupt bureaucrats of the government or regional authority. Women who sign up to the movement may be rewarded morally and materially: they receive the respect accorded to the 'mothers of the believers' while benefiting from the organization's welfare programmes. In Islam as Protestantism and Judaism, God may be seen to reward those who abide by His rules.

There is, of course, a negative side to this picture. The benefits of sexual virtue are purchased at a formidable moral cost. In the polarized, Manichaean world of fundamentalist discourse, virtue is not enough. The enemies of God must be demonized. The 'loose' woman is an agent of Satan. In fundamentalist tracts 'family values' becomes a code-word for homophobia. At least half the literature put out by 'Focus on the Family', a lobby group based in Colorado, is dedicated to denunciations of homosexuality. James Robison, the American televangelist, sees homosexuals as being in the same class as rapists, bank robbers, and murderers. 'You don't have to trouble yourself about whether it is normal to be a homosexual.'[24] Yet it is rarely, if ever, explained how homosexuality threatens or undermines family values. (Indeed, the opposite seems truer:

gays often remain closer to their parents than children who marry and leave home.) Fundamentalist fear of homosexuality has crossed the Atlantic, invading the Church of England, in which a significant proportion of clergy is gay. According to one diocesan bishop homosexuality is caused by 'demons in the anus'.[25] In the summer of 2003 the appointment of Dr Jeffrey John, an openly gay clergyman, as Bishop of Reading and his subsequent withdrawal under pressure from bishops in Africa and evangelicals within the Church became a major source of controversy threatening a permanent split in the Anglican communion.

Similar trends are found in the world of Islam, where the traditional tolerance of homosexuality as being less threatening to 'family values' than heterosexual (especially female) infidelity is now being replaced by active homophobia, with homosexuality stereotyped (quite inaccurately) as an 'imported' Western vice. Fresh from their all-male seminaries, the Taliban who ruled in Afghanistan executed homosexuals by lapidation, bulldozing walls to crush their bodies. In Iran, after the revolution, homosexuals were hanged; in Egypt, under fundamentalist pressure, discos frequented by gays have been closed down and participants arrested.

In all such instances, fundamentalist concern to maintain the family as a social unit and transmitter of conservative values has been overtaken by a neurotic obsession with sexual behaviour. Space does not allow for a lengthy speculation into the causes of fundamentalist homophobia at this point: but it seems obvious that self-repression and fear of one's own 'inner demons' or sexual impulses have much to do with it. The work of two scholars, Howard Eilberg-Schwartz and Brenda Brasher, suggests a plausible line of enquiry. The origins of homophobia in the Judaeo-Christian tradition may lie in the 'contradictory religious ethos' experienced by devout Christian males. On the one hand they are expected to love a solitary deity imagined in terms both of father imagery, and perhaps more potently, through the erotically charged figure of a young, almost naked male impaled on an instrument of torment. On the other they inherit from the Hebrews and other ancient peoples for whom childbearing was a 'civic duty linked to survival', the idea of 'heterosexuality as a highly valued social norm'.[26] Catholicism masks this contradiction through the institution of celibacy in its clergy, a symbolic 'third sex' that dresses in female garb and seems disproportionately liable to indulge in male paedophilia, to judge from recent scandals involving child abuse in the Church. At the same time the danger posed by the homoerotic love of Jesus is mitigated for Catholics by devotion to his mother, a figure who is conspicuously absent from the varieties of 'macho' Protestantism exported from America. When homoerotic feelings clash with heterosexual values, homophobia (directed against those who acknowledge and give expression to such forbidden sentiments) provides an all too obvious and easy way out.

The same line of reasoning, in the Judaeo-Christian, if not the Islamic, context (where the deity is less likely to be imagined anthropomorphically, and where the Prophet Muhammad is imagined as a heterosexually robust male) suggests why fundamentalist churches or movements may appeal especially to women. After a detailed examination of women in two fundamentalist churches in southern California, Brenda Brasher concludes that despite their exclusion from official positions of authority 'fundamentalist women can and do exercise considerable power in the religious institutions they join'.[27]

Facing a myriad of unresolved conflicts among the quintuple roles of wife, mother, wage earner, housekeeper and citizen ... [fundamentalist] women are opting for involvement in religious communities that support them in the role of believer, which relativizes all other demands upon the self. Before anything else ... [such] women are people of faith, committed to their relationship with God.[28]

The priority they give to their religious life enables these women to deal with the contradictions they experience in a society in which self-esteem is supposed to be achieved through work, 'but workplaces do not deal with the female body as normative', in a nation whose public rhetoric insists that family values are paramount while actually providing 'a social environment where parenting largely remains the responsibility of women, where commitments to parenting are not valued, where education is absurdly underfunded and where child care grossly inadequate'.[29] Their overarching religious commitment and the female support they find in their churches makes it easier for women to cope with lives that are full of tensions and difficulties. The very emphasis on male authority in congregational and domestic life has its advantages for such women. Marriage is valued, sexual fidelity demanded, drinking and carousing—traditional male pursuits—discouraged. Men are expected to take an active part in bringing up their children.[30] As Frances Fitzgerald observed: 'To tell "Dad" that he made all the decisions might be a small price to pay to get the father of your children to become a respectable middle-class citizen.'[31]

Viewed from this perspective female fundamentalism—which is found in all traditions—may be a transitional phase between the world in which women were largely confined to the home and one in which they fully participate in public and business life. Anita Weiss, who has worked with Muslim women in a traditionalist social milieu in Lahore, Pakistan, concludes that while the men view their womenfolk as being more capable than in the past, they also feel threatened by the potential of 'uncontrolled, educated and economically independent women to compromise their honour and therefore their status among other men'.[32] The anthropologist Michael Gilsenan draws similar conclusions from his work in northern Lebanon. '*Sharaf*, the honour of person and family which is particularly identified with control of women's sexuality, is crucial to the public, social identity of men.'[33] Fundamentalisms are dynamic movements in the contemporary social landscape. Though conservative, they are far from being static. Nor are they uniformly reactionary. By formally accepting male authority when moving into public arenas formerly the preserve of males, fundamentalist women hope to soothe men's anxieties while quietly taking over their jobs.

5

Fundamentalism and Nationalism I

> The New Englanders are a People of God settled in
> those places which were once the Devil's territories
> ... a People here accomplishing the promise of old
> made unto our Blessed Jesus, that He would have the
> Utmost parts of the Earth for His possession.
>
> (Cotton Mather, New England Puritan)[1]

The Puritan settlers in America would not have seen
themselves as 'fundamentalists' since the term had not yet
been invented. Fundamentalism only comes into being
when challenged by modernist theologies, when post-
Enlightenment scholarship is perceived as threatening to
the eternal verities enshrined in the Word. But the
American Puritans were fundamentalist in a broader
sense in that they understood the portions of the Bible in a
way that differed significantly from most of their old-world
counterparts. Whereas Bunyan's *Pilgrim's Progress* would

express the Puritan spirit allegorically, his 'City of Destruction' and 'Slough of Despond' being convincing depictions of psychological states in the 'wilderness of this world', the American pilgrim experienced his biblical narratives concretely, especially the Book of Exodus, which charts the deliverance of the Children of Israel out of Egypt. There is a one-to-one correspondence between miraculous crossing of the Red Sea by the Israelites led by Moses, and the *Mayflower*'s perilous journey across the Atlantic. The New Jerusalem promised in the Book of Revelation—a spiritual aspiration for William Blake—was for Joseph Smith, the Mormon Prophet, a Zion of bricks and mortar where the Kingdom of God acquired material form.

'The destiny of the American People is to subdue the continent, to unite the world in one social family,' wrote William Gilpin, Governor of Colorado Territory, in 1846. 'Divine task! Immortal mission! America leads the host of nations as they ascend to this order of civilization ... the industrial conquest of the world.'[2] It is not customary to speak of 'American nationalism' but there can be little doubt that the 'fundamentals' of Christianity, as they came to be understood by evangelical American Protestants in the twentieth century, were closely bound up with the construction of a core WASP (White Anglo-Saxon Protestant) identity that sought to preserve itself from dissolution by 'external' influences, ranging from imported German scholarship, Catholic immigration, and socialism, equated with communism—not to mention the profane cultural influences emanating from Hollywood, which was seen to be dominated by emancipated, non-religious Jews. On the domestic front, moreover, most fundamentalists avoided having to engage in social interaction with the descendants of African slaves. The fundamentalist Southern Baptist Convention (comprising some 40,000 independent churches) is overwhelmingly white; while Bob Jones University, a fundamentalist educational bastion, still applies archaic rules against mixed racial dating. While some scholars see fundamentalism and nationalism as rival ideologies, in America, as in Israel, the movements are often barely distinguishable. '"Faith in the Nation" though it still resonates through socially conservative, militarily-connected networks inside and outside the United States, has been appropriated in a symbolic sense by the fundamentalists. It justifies their role in realising global evangelization and revitalizing Americanism.'[3]

American fundamentalists perceive no conflict between religion and patriotism. Like their Puritan predecessors, they identify America with Israel as a land covenanted to God's People on condition that they followed God's laws. The televangelist Pat Robertson (who unsuccessfully stood as a candidate for nomination as the Republican Party's presidential candidate in 1987) is quite explicit about this identification. America remained the world's greatest and most powerful country so long as it kept God's commandments. Since the Supreme Court 'insulted God' by

BOX 16

In 1350 BC the great lawgiver Moses gave his people one final instruction before his own death and their entry into the Promised Land ... Wonderful blessings were specified to the nation if it would diligently 'obey the voice of the Lord your God, to keep His commandments ...'. As we review the history of the United States, it is clear that every one of those promises made to ancient Israel has come true here as well. There has never been in the history of the world any nation more powerful, more free, or more generously endowed with physical possessions ... We have more wealth than the richest of all empires. We have had more military might than any colossus. We have risen above all the nations of the earth ... America has led the world in science, in medicine, in technology, in agriculture, in tele-communications, in industrial production, in banking, in trade, and in overall gross national product ... Our individual freedoms are legendary, and our democratic processes have set the standard for nations throughout the world that are struggling to throw off the shackles of slavery and move into ordered liberty. But these things did not happen by accident, nor did they happen somehow because the citizens of America are smarter or more worthy than the citizens of any other country. It happened because those men and women who founded this land made a solemn covenant that they would be the people of God and that this would be a Christian nation.

(Pat Robertson, *The Turning Tide: The Fall of Liberalism and the Rise of Common Sense*)

banning prayer in school, America has been defeated in war, one president has been assassinated and another forced to resign, foreign powers have amassed huge surpluses in their trade with America, and the country is mired in debt. Since the Supreme Court 'legalized murder' by extending abortion rights, the country has been at the mercy of the OPEC oil cartel, American children have been 'victimized by marijuana, heroin, hallucinogens, crack cocaine, glue, PCP, alcohol, unbridled sex, a pop music culture that has destroyed their minds, the occult and Hindu holy men, and an epidemic of disease'. Only a return to God can save the nation.[4]

Despite the very different social and political contexts of America and the Islamic worlds, the arguments are similar to those deployed by Islamist writers and preachers. The Prophet Muhammad, according to this argument, triumphed over his enemies through battle as well as by preaching. Building on his victories as well as his obedience to God, his successors, the Rightly Guided Caliphs, conquered most of West Asia and North Africa as well as Spain. In this view the truth of Islam was vindicated on the plane of real-time history, through its historical achievement in creating what would become a great world civilization. The decline of Islam is directly attributable to loss of faith by Muslims and especially Muslim rulers who do not rule in accordance with Islamic law. If Muslims and leaders return to the 'straight path' of righteousness ordained by God, the social and political decline that resulted in colonialism and the shabby, corrupt post-colonial order will be reversed. Far from being counter-nationalist, as argued by some scholars and ideologists, the fundamentalist argument that God rewards righteousness in terms of national success and this-worldly prosperity is one that chimes in well with nationalist aims.

Theoretically, fundamentalism and nationalism are ideological opponents. For Bruce Lawrence nationalism is essentially an outcome of the industrial revolution and the progressive modernist ideologies that emerged from it. 'All fundamentalists are ideologues protesting the modernist hegemony in the High Tech Era ... The arch-enemy of fundamentalism is not bi-culturalism but nationalism.'[5] In the formal discourses of writers such as Abul Ala Mawdudi, one the most influential Islamist writers, religion stands at 'the polar opposite of nationalism and all that nationalism stands for'.[6] Nationalism, for Maududi, promotes popular sovereignty or the 'will of the people' expressed through secular institutions such as parliaments or national assemblies which legislate for the nation. 'The principle of the Unity of God', he wrote, 'altogether negates the concept of the legal and political sovereignty of human beings, individually or collectively ... God alone is sovereign and His commandments are the Law of Islam.'[7] Maududi's opposition to nationalism was not just based on the fear that the Indian Muslim community from which he came would be discriminated against or suffer loss of identity in a Hindu-majority state: he was equally opposed to Muslim nationalism which he saw as being 'as reprehensible in the Sharia (law) of God as Indian nationalism'.[8] According to Lawrence, Islamic fundamentalists generally have 'refused the opiate of any nationalism as the cure for failed Islamic idealism. They have taken an unequivocal stance against Arab, Persian, Turkish, Pakistani, Malay and Indonesian nationalisms.'[9]

In Arab countries especially, according to this argument, the Islamist movements are ideological competitors of Arab nationalists. They aim to replace them in government, whether by winning elections (as in Algeria in 1991) or by armed rebellion, as happened in the Egyptian city of Assiut following the assassination of President Anwar Sadat in October 1981 and in the Syrian city of Hama where at least 10,000 people were killed after a rebellion by the Muslim Brotherhood in 1982. Islamist ideologues regularly denounce their nationalist competitors or rulers as 'infidels' or 'man worshippers', as usurpers who have substituted man-made laws instead of instituting the 'rule of God'. The theocracies they advocate are supposed to be incompatible with human government.

In practice the situation is rather more complicated. Historically, nationalisms in Europe emerged with the rise of urban autonomy and the 'emancipation of the bourgeoisie' from feudal bonds, sometimes in alliance with monarchs against landed aristocracies, sometimes against them. Both the French and American revolutions generated nationalist forces by extending 'bourgeois free-

BOX 17

Nationalism was first of all a doctrine of popular freedom and sovereignty. The people must be liberated—that is, free from an external constraint; they must determine their own destiny and be masters in their own house; they must control their own resources; they must obey only their own 'inner' voice. But that entailed fraternity. The people must be united; they must dissolve all internal divisions; they must be gathered together in a single historic territory, a homeland; and they must have legal equality and share a single public culture. But which culture and what territory? Only a homeland that was 'theirs' by historic right, the land of their forebears; only a culture that was 'theirs' as a heritage, passed down the generations, and therefore an expression of their authentic identity.

(John Hutchinson and Anthony D. Smith (eds), *Nationalism*)

doms' with all the rights of citizenship to the whole of society (though not, in America's case, to slaves). In France, as in Russia after 1917, the revolution took a radically anti-clerical turn, because of the Church's strong identification with the discredited *ancien régime*. After 1792 the French Revolution, with its popular assemblies, processions, and fêtes, began exporting its patriotic ideals throughout Europe. Napoleon's conquests catalysed the forces of nationalism in Europe by provoking patriotic responses in Britain, Spain, Germany, Poland, and

Russia—if not in Italy, where the anti-papal nationalism of the Risorgimento took longer to come to fruition.

It would be wrong, however, to see nationalism as being uniformly anti-religious and secular. Everywhere nationalisms have been permeated by religious symbols, especially in places where the core identities that came to constitute nationhood had been buttressed by religious differences. The different identities that made up Britain were sustained by Presbyterianism in Scotland, non-conformity in Wales, and Catholicism in Ireland (excepting the North)—just as Polish and Croatian identities were sustained by Catholicism; Greek and Serb identities by Eastern Orthodoxy; Malayan (or Malaysian) by Islam; Tibetan, Thai, and Sri Lankan identities by Buddhism. Yet for every case where national and religious allegiances seem to run in tandem, there are also contradictions. The Russian patriotism that gloried in the achievements of Peter the Great also contained Slavophile elements which 'harked back to pre-Petrine Muscovy and its Orthodox monastic ways' at a time of incipient industrialization and capitalism.[10] The movement for Greek independence from the Ottomans, inspired by the French Revolution and Romantics such as Byron, combined two contradictory elements: a 'bourgeois' constituency of merchants and intelligentsia who sought to revive the glories of ancient Athens (a mood expressed in the neoclassical designs imported from Bavaria by the young King Otto, whom the Greek notables chose as their monarch on the strength of his father King Ludwig I's interest in neoclassicism); and a pious stratum among the Orthodox clergy and peasants who yearned for the recovery of Constantinople and the Byzantine Empire. The pan-Hellenic nationalism that surfaced in the twentieth century under Eleftherios Venizelos is not usually thought of as 'fundamentalism': but in the final analysis the romantic impulse behind the quest for lost greatness, for the recovery of divinely-ordered empire, may be the same for Greeks as for Arabs and Muslims.

The ideal Islamic order aspired to by modern Islamist ideologues, including Abbassi Madani, the principal leader and founder of the Islamic Salvation Front (FIS) in Algeria, the Saudi dissident Osama bin Laden and the followers of the late Sheikh Taqi al-Din al-Nabahani, founder of the Islamic Liberation Party, Hizb al-Tahrir, corresponds to the classical concept of the Caliphate, just as Venizelos harked back to the glory of Constantinople. In the Arab case defeat at the hands of Israel in successive wars helped to popularize the quest for lost grandeur, a compensatory mechanism, perhaps, for failure on the battlefield. The revival of the Islamist movement in Egypt, quiescent during the heyday of Gamal Abdul Nasser, dates from Egypt's catastrophic defeat by Israel in 1967—the moment when the modernist agenda behind his brand of his 'secular' Arab nationalism with its socialist orientation was discredited. But to state that the Arab nationalism articulated by Nasser and the Islamism or 'fundamentalism' of Bin Laden, Madani, and Nabahani are ideologically distinct

•

The power of a government did not operate uniformly within a fixed and generally recognized area, as happened in Europe, but rather radiated 'from a number of urban centers with a force which tended to grow weaker with distance and with the existence of natural or human obstacles'.[11] Patriotism was focused, not as in Renaissance Italy, England, or Holland, on the city, city-state, or nation in the modern territorial sense, but on the clan or tribe within the larger unit of the Umma, the worldwide Islamic community. Local solidarities were reinforced by practices such as marriage between first cousins, a requirement in many communities. Clan loyalties were further buttressed by religion, with tribal leaders justifying their rebellions or wars of conquest by appealing to the defence of true Islam against its infidel enemies. An example is that of the 'fundamentalist' leader Ibn Saud, a tribal leader who conquered, and united, most of the Arabian peninsular between 1904 and 1926 in alliance with a movement for religious reform founded by an eighteenth-century cleric, Muhammad ibn Abd al-Wahhab. The Wahhabi movement, which is still highly influential, thanks to the petrodollars it receives from its Saudi patrons, is counternationalist in the sense that it sees its mission as universal and does not confine itself within the territorial boundaries of the Saudi state. Like other 'fundamentalist' movements such as the Muslim Brotherhood (with whom it forged close ideological ties from the 1960s) it aims to revitalize the whole of the Umma along Wahhabi fundamentalist lines. But in a broader sense it conforms to what Mark Juergensmeyer prefers to call 'religious nationalism'. Just as 'secular nationalism' is far from being devoid of religious content, so 'religious nationalism' is primarily political.

Unlike Lawrence, Juergensmeyer does not see nationalism as the ideological or polar opposite of 'fundamentalism', but rather as its complement or variant. To expand somewhat on his argument, the nationalism that originated in Europe with the consolidation of national states such as England, France, Germany, and Italy became universal after the Second World War when former colonies everywhere demanded, and mostly won, their independence. The spread of nationalism across the globe was the outcome not only of European history, but also of American support for the principle of self-determination famously enunciated by US President Woodrow Wilson at the end of the First World War. From 1945 it was greatly assisted by the United Nations, which promoted decolonization and encouraged the creation of national states by conferring legitimacy on new members. The process of national formation, by which the globe was formatted into discrete territorial units on the European model, was further assisted by international bodies such as the World Bank and IMF (International Monetary Fund), which boosted the financial control of national governments; by security and economic pacts such as SEATO (South East Asian Treaty Organization) and ASEAN (Association of

South East Asian Nations) and by political measures to control the manufacture and sale of weaponry in order to ensure that internationally recognized governments would monopolize the means of violence. (In areas of contested sovereignty such as South-East Asia and the Middle East, the arming of rivals, of course, helped to encourage wars.)

National leaders such as Jawaharlal Nehru of India, Gamal Abdul Nasser of Egypt, and Ahmed Sukarno of Indonesia subscribed to versions of secular nationalism which provided them with constituencies and power bases over the heads of 'traditional' religious or ethnic leaders. In Egypt, North Africa, and most of the Middle East, this type of 'secular' nationalism was not perceived as being anti-religious, though one version, Baathism, held an appeal for religious minorities, since one of its founders was Christian and its outlook was explicitly anti-sectarian. The mainstream versions of Arab nationalism that emerged in the course of the anti-colonial struggles against the British and French incorporated important elements of the reformist agenda of the *salafiya* movement founded by Jamal al-Din al-Afghani, often regarded as the first 'Islamic fundamentalist', and his disciple Muhammad Abduh in the 1880s. In India Nehru was heir to the independence movement led by Mahatma Gandhi, who incorporated Hindu elements of renunciation and sacrifice into his theory of Satyaghraha ('truth-force' or 'active non-violence'); while in Indonesia the ideology of Pancasila or 'five principles' promoted by Sukarno combined belief in monotheism with themes considered acceptable to the country's Christian, Buddhist, and Hindu minorities. As in Southern Ireland, these new nationalisms went with the grain of religious feeling.

In the early post-independence years secular nationalism was not yet seen as being in conflict with the religious variety, although conflicts would emerge in due course. The Muslim Brotherhood, founded in Egypt in 1928, could be described as a culturally nationalist organization which sought to eliminate Western cultural influences, such as alcohol consumption and the free mixing of sexes, and to revitalize Islam as an essential part of the project for national renewal. The Brotherhood collaborated with more secular-minded nationalists in their opposition to the establishment of a Jewish state in Palestine and to the presence of British troops in the Suez Canal zone. When the old-style Egyptian nationalists of the Wafd Party (named after the hoped-for delegation (*wafd*) Britain refused to allow Egypt to send to the Paris Peace Conference in 1919) were discredited for their collaboration with Britain during the Second World War and blamed for Egypt's defeat by the new state of Israel in 1948, the Brotherhood joined hands with Arab nationalists (or pan-Arabists) to destabilize the government by means of popular riots and demonstrations, a movement which culminated in the military *coup d'état* which overthrew the monarchy in July 1952. As Paul Berman points out,

BOX 18

'Both movements dreamed of rescuing the Arab world from the legacies of European imperialism. Both groups dreamed of crushing Zionism and the brand-new Jewish state. Both groups dreamed of fashioning a new kind of modernity, which was not going to be liberal and freethinking in the Western style but, even so, was going to be up-to-date on economic and scientific issues. And both movements dreamed of doing all this by returning in some fashion to the glories of the Arab past. Both movements wanted to resurrect, in a modern version, the ancient Islamic caliphate of the seventh century, when the Arabs were conquering the world.'[12]

(Paul Berman, 'The Philosopher of Islamic Terror', *New York Times Magazine*, 23 Mar. 2003)[12]

the pan-Arabists around Gamal Abdul Nasser and the Muslim Brothers held much in common:

The initial falling out that occurred between Nasser and the Brotherhood after the revolution was as much about power as it was about ideology. The Brotherhood felt cheated of its right to lead the revolution and resorted to violence. After an attempt on Nasser's life in 1954 the Egyptian leader forced the movement underground. Later, supported by King Faisal of Saudi Arabia, the Brotherhood exported its luminaries and became caught up in the conflict between the 'progressive' Arab forces sponsored by

Egypt and the 'conservatives' supported by Saudi Arabia. Under pressure of persecution in Egypt, the movement became divided between the pragmatists who were prepared to work within the political system (even though technically the organization remained banned) and the radicals who formulated various doctrines aimed at justifying the seizure of power by violent means.

Juergensmeyer, following Mircea Eliade, sees secular nationalism as itself having many of the characteristics of a religion, including doctrine, myth, ethics, ritual experience, and social organization. 'This structural similarity between secular nationalism and religion is complemented by what I regard as an even more basic, functional similarity: they both serve the ethical function of providing an overarching framework of moral order, a framework that commands ultimate loyalty from those who subscribe to it.' The strongest parallel, he concludes, lies in the 'ability of nationalism and religion, alone among all forms of allegiance, to give moral sanction to martyrdom and violence'.[13]

The interconnected, overlapping relationship between secular and religious nationalisms is particularly evident where Islamist movements have taken power or come close to exercising it. In Algeria the Islamic Salvation Front (FIS) was forced underground after the army intervened in December 1991 to prevent it from winning the second round of the national elections. Prior to its dismantling, the Front was a coalition of two main groupings: the *salafi* group, whose leaders were mostly educated through the medium of Arabic in Algeria or outside the country in the Arab East or English-speaking countries; and the Francophone al-Jazara group, or 'Algerianists', who were considered more open to modernist influences. Both factions were united in their desire to establish a state based on a restoration of the Islamic law, although according to the Paris-based Algerian journalist Ahmed Rouadjia, 'al-Jazara offers a much less rigid reading of Islam than the salafi school, which is attached to the spirit and the letter of the Quran'.[14] Both groups rejected democracy as *kufr* (disbelief), and as a concept that is 'semantically alien to the spirit and texts, both sacred and secular, of Islam'. The denunciations of democracy by FIS leaders was one of the pretexts the army was able to use for the overthrow of President Chadli Benjadid after the FIS victory at the polls in November 1991. One of the main beneficiaries of the army's action, which unleashed a cruel and bloody civil war that is said to have cost at least 100,000 lives, were Hamas (not to be confused with the Palestinian movement of the same name) and Nahda, two moderate Islamist parties that shared the cultural aims of FIS but were prepared to work within the system. The divisions among the Islamists enabled the President Zeroual and his successor Abd al-Aziz Bouteflika to reintroduce limited democracy with a measure of Islamist support.

The merging of Islamist and 'Algerianist', or nationalist, currents in Algeria is consistent with patterns in many other Arab countries where the Islamist movements are challenging authoritarian or military-based regimes. Theoretically, in its 'pure' or 'ideal-typical' forms, Islamism may present itself as an ideological alternative to nationalism, which it sometimes describes as a manifestation of *kufr*. But as in Ireland, where nationalists are almost invariably Catholic and loyalists invariably Protestant, the realities are much more complex. Opposition forces, whether nationalist or Islamist, feed on common discontents and manifest a common desire for a more 'authentic' national culture. In their militant forms they exhibit the same intolerance for lifestyles deemed to be immoral or imported. Both attack the corruption of the military-backed regimes they seek to supplant. Both attack nationalisms they regard as discredited. As Rouadjia explains: 'Over thirty years of independence, marked by speeches full of glory and heroism, the people had come to understand that the "nationalism" in question was just a tragic farce whose first victims were precisely those who had believed in it.'[15] But while challenging the old-style nationalism of the incumbent elites, Islamists adopt many of their assumptions. As Laura Guazzone points out, Islamists, for all the differences between them, share two basic convictions. The first is that the Sharia, the Islamic religious law, 'provides a comprehensive and organic system for the regulation of all aspects of human life—individual, social and political—in accordance with God's will'. The second is that a 'society of good Muslims can

the state as the central framework of Islamist political thinking and action constitutes a signal departure from theories of government developed during the classical age of Islam. It 'is clearly the result of dialectics with the cultural antagonists of Islamism—liberalism, nationalism and socialism—and of the engagement of the Islamist movements in *national* political processes'.[17]

The results are paradoxical. Where Islamists have actually held power as (briefly, at municipal level) in Algeria, in Iran since the 1979 'Islamic' revolution, and in Sudan since 1989, it is the post-colonial state and the interest groups controlling it that have benefited, rather than civil society. The rhetorical appeal of political Islam as representing 'freedom, under God, from the dominion of man over man'—the source of its capacity to mobilize people against tyrannical regimes—produces machia-vellian-style pragmatism that can prove to be no less corrupt or authoritarian than the system it replaces. The new regime's stated priorities may change from promising economic development and increasing prosperity to defending private virtue and public morality. The shift in emphasis from economics to morality may be to the advantage of free enterprise while appealing to the values of recently urbanized rural immigrants and the religiously observant middle class of small businessmen and shop-keepers, the two groups which constitute the backbone of Islamist support. In the case of Iran, and to a lesser extent the Sudan, the Islamist conquest of the state may have increased political participation, by enfranchising previously excluded or marginal groups. But far from diminishing the purchase of an oppressive authoritarian state over society, the Islamists have achieved the opposite, intentionally or otherwise. The shift from state control over the economy to state enforcement of social morality involves no diminution in the state's actual power—rather the reverse.

The most explicit statement of this paradox appears in a letter the Ayatollah Khomeini wrote in January 1988, shortly before his death, to the man who succeeded him as the Supreme Guide of the Islamic Republic, the then President Ali Khamenei. Khomeini ruled that the power of the Islamic Republic was comparable to that enjoyed by the Prophet Muhammad himself. It was thereby permitted to take any measures in the interests of the Islamic state even where these might conflict with Islamic law as traditionally interpreted, including the religious obligations of prayer, fasting during the holy month of Ramadan, or Hajj (pilgrimage to Mecca). By giving the state priority over Islamic law Khomeini revealed his true colours. Far from being a 'traditionalist' he established the theological ground for a radical break in the traditional relationship between Islam and the state, according to which the ruler was supposed to 'govern in accordance with what God sent down' (i.e. the Koran and the legal system derived from it) and to subject himself to these laws.

In post-Khomeini Iran state power is as formidable as it

was before 1979 during the authoritarian regime of the Shah. A reformist parliament which generally supports the elected president, the liberally inclined cleric Ali Khatami, is frustrated in its efforts to liberalize the social agenda by the conservative clerics who control the Council of Guardians and the judiciary. Students, writers, and politicians who dare to challenge the clerical rule are harassed, tortured, imprisoned, and in some cases sentenced to death.

In the case of Sudan, where the Islamists came to power on the back of the military coup in June 1989 by General Omar al-Bashir, the state has extended its powers in the name of Islam. General Bashir, following the example of his predecessor Jaafar al-Nimairi, brought the leader of the National Islamic Front (NIF), the suave, urbane, Sorbonne-educated Hasan al-Turabi into government, enabling him to become the ideological force behind his regime. The Islamization measures introduced by Nimairi under Turabi's influence alienated the non-Muslim South, provoking Africa's longest-running civil war. When in June 1989 the democratically elected government that followed the fall of Nimairi suspended the Islamic laws as a prelude to peace negotiations, it was overthrown by Bashir, supported by a clique of Islamist officers. The war against the South was a *jihad* which had to be continued for the glory of Allah. Non-Christians such as the Nuer and Dinka peoples were subjected to forcible conversion. The Nuba Mountains region, especially, has been the target of ethnic cleansing by the northern

Sudanese, with measures such as 'the confiscation of land, the eradication of whole communities, the destruction of entire villages, the enslavement of children and the torture and murder of Nuba people regardless of age and sex'.[18] Bashir was able to use the NIF's programme, which included purges and executions of non-Islamists in the top ranks of the army and civil service, to smash the power of the traditional political parties, dominated by the Sufi (mystical) brotherhoods and the Ansar, descendants of the Baqqara and other tribes which supported the *jihad* of the Mahdi Muhammad Ahmad against the Anglo-Egyptian conquest in the 1880s and 1890s. The NIF compensated for its lack of mass support by recruiting tribesmen from the Fallata, a previously marginal group of West Africans 'whose loyalty and willingness to do the government's dirty work were all the more fervent because they risked forfeiting everything should the NIF lose its grip on power'.[19] Ten years into the dictatorship, Turabi had served his purpose. In December 1999 the General ousted Turabi from power in a 'palace coup'.

Far from being counter-nationalist in the sense of opposing the 'secular' national states imposed on the Islamic world since decolonization, Islamism in practice mostly reveals itself as an alternative variety of nationalism whose political focus is cultural and religious rather than primarily economic (although Islamists do have some economic theories such as interest-free banking, which have been implemented in some Muslim countries with varied degrees of success). In the Palestinian territories occupied by Israel since 1967 the Islamist groups Hamas and Islamic Jihad have shown more nationalist fervour than the more secular-oriented Palestinian Liberation Organization (PLO) by engaging in acts of terror such as suicide bombings in metropolitan Israel specifically aimed at sabotaging the peace process in which the PLO has been engaged. In Pakistan the Islamist Jamaat-i-Islami was fervently nationalistic in supporting the army's brutal campaign (which involved the systematic mass rape of Bengali women by soldiers mainly from the Punjab) against the secessionist movement in East Pakistan that resulted in the formation of Bangladesh.

In theory there remains a contradiction between the utopian aim of a restored universal Islamic caliphate shared by supporters of Osama bin Laden and Sheikh Nabahani. In practice, the logic of circumstances and the interplay of local ethnicities and regional rivalries ensure that the energies of Islamist movements are directed towards the attainment of power within existing Muslim states or communities, even though Islamists, like Arab nationalists before them, resent the presence of international boundaries separating them from their 'brethren' and dream of reuniting the Umma under a revived universal caliphate.

6

Fundamentalism and Nationalism II

'The object of every national movement is only the seeking for its god, who must be its own god, and the faith in him as the only true one. God is the synthetic personality of the whole people taken from its beginning to its end' wrote Fyodor Dostoyevsky in *The Possessed*. The same insight informs the religious sociology of Emil Durkheim, who equated the sacred with the spirit of community, a projection of the communal spirit onto a supernatural, transcendental Being. Like religious communities, the nations are collectivities that transcend the sum of their individual parts; like religious communities nations bear witness to the idea that human blood must be shed in their defence: the war memorials, cenotaphs, and Tombs to the Unknown Warrior that grace our cities attest to transcendental demands the nation makes of its citizens. Such demands, as Anthony Smith points out, are made on the basis of faith rather than empirical evidence. 'For nationalists, the nation, whatever the acts committed in its name, is essentially and ultimately good, as the future will reveal; the conviction of its virtue is not a matter of empirical evidence, but of faith.'[1]

Nationalist rhetoric everywhere is suffused with religious symbolism and purpose. To give but one example, let me cite some extracts from the address by the Irish patriot Padraic Pearse, architect of the 1916 rebellion against Britain, at the graveside of an earlier nationalist, the Fenian Jeremiah O'Donovan Rossa in August 1915: Pearse declares that he is speaking 'on behalf of a new generation that has been re-baptised in the Fenian faith, and that has accepted the responsibility of carrying out the Fenian programme'. He goes on to propose 'that, here by the grave of this unrepentant Fenian, we renew our baptismal vows ... We stand at Rossa's grave not in sadness but rather in exaltation of spirit that it has been given to us to come thus into so close a communion with that brave and splendid Gael. Splendid and holy causes are served by men who are themselves splendid and holy.' The language is the language of religion ('baptism', 'exaltation', 'communion', 'holy', 'spirit'), not the empirical language of politics.[2]

As suggested in the previous chapter, the biblical story of Exodus exercised a powerful influence on the construction of American identities, from the Pilgrim Fathers to the New Zions (Nauvoo, Illinois, and Salt Lake City, Utah) founded by the Mormon Prophet Joseph Smith and his successor Brigham Young ('The American Moses') in

BOX 19

This little province has had the peculiar preservation of divine Providence. You only have to read the history of Ulster to see that time after time when it seemed humanly impossible to extricate Ulster from seeming disaster, that God intervened. Why? God has a purpose for this province, and this plant of Protestantism sown here in the north-eastern part of this island. The enemy has tried to root it out, but it still grows today, and I believe, like a grain of mustard seed its future is going to be mightier yet. God Who made her mighty will make her mightier yet in His Divine will.

(Ian Paisley in Steve Bruce, *God Save Ulster: The Religion and Politics of Paisleysim*)

the American West during the 1840s. Taken to heart by Bible-loving Protestants, the Exodus myth has buttressed the group identities of Scottish-Irish Protestants in Ulster and Afrikaaners in Southern Africa. In addition to the familiar enactment or exploitation of this myth by European Protestants, Anthony Smith has shown how the biblical idea of a 'chosen people' modelled on the Israelites was a vital component in the religious outlook of peoples as diverse as Ethiopian and Armenians.

For Jews the Exodus narrative is not just treated historically but ritualized and given a spiritual meaning. According to Rabbi Sybil Sheridan all Jews at the Seder table at Passover 'are to think of the Exodus as if they too were in Egypt at that time, and all are understood to have stood at the foot of Mount Sinai and been witness to the theophany that there took place'.[3] It is not so much the event in itself that is central to the belief, but its meaning and the reinforcement of meaning through symbols and celebrations, especially in orthodox Judaism which tends to approach history (or, to be more accurate, historical mythology) thematically rather than 'historically'. The themes of exile and return, sin and repentance, are demonstrated again and again in the Bible, from the creation to the end of time.[4] The theologian Rudolf Bultmann credits the notion that history has meaning and purpose to the Jews and Christians, whose understanding of history depended on eschatology: 'The Greeks did not raise the question of meaning in history and the ancient philosophers had not developed a philosophy of history. A philosophy of history grew up for the first time in Christian thinking, for Christians believed they knew of the end of the world and of history.' Bultmann concludes that the idea of historical progress that appears in the writings of Hegel and Marx is really a secularized version of Christian eschatology. 'Hegel and Marx, each in his own way, believed they knew the goal of history and interpreted the course of history in the light of this presupposed goal.'[5]

Jewish nationalism or Zionism actualizes the eschatological expectations surrounding the coming of the Messiah by de-supernaturalizing the Redeemer, placing the destiny of Israel in human hands. Most Jewish people regard themselves as descendants of the ancient Hebrew occupants of Palestine. Whether or not one regards such claims as sustainable in the face of historical and genetic evidence to the contrary, the idea of Jewish ethnicity is underpinned by the religion, with Jewish identity predicated on a religious tradition extending back to antiquity. The Zionist movement secularized that tradition, without providing an unchallengeable notion of secular 'Jewishness'. (The legal question of 'Who is a Jew' has kept the Supreme Court of Israel busy for decades.) The founder of modern Zionism, Theodor Herzl, was a secular Jew who wanted his state to be as 'Jewish' as 'England is English'— at a time when England was much more ethnically homogeneous than it is today. The '-ish' attached to Jew embraces a broad spectrum of possible identities, from the almost complete assimilation within the majority communities, to the radical separatism of some of the Israeli Haredim who redesignate themselves as 'true' Jews in a world of 'gentile' Israelis whose claim to Jewishness they regard as inauthentic.

Jewish ritual is centred on the myth of Exodus and the stories of the Jews in their ancient homeland. Before the Nazi Holocaust, however, the greeting 'Next Year in Jerusalem' used by worshippers on High Holidays was usually understood symbolically or prophetically, as a hope to be deferred to the end of time. When political Zionists began transforming the messianic promise of redemption into a practical programme in the late nineteenth century, their religious leaders were appalled. The yearning for Zion, they argued, was a spiritual longing, to be assuaged only at the eschaton or end of days, when the Messiah would come and restore the land of Israel to its rightful owners. To turn this religious vision into a political reality was both foolish and blasphemous. Some orthodox rabbis went so far as to excommunicate the Zionists. However perilous the situation facing Jewish communities in Europe, especially those living under Russian rule, the Zionist solution was unacceptable. If the Zionists had their way Jewish life would be directed away from religious observance and the study of holy texts, towards a political project outside the control of the rabbis.

'Secular' Zionism had a nationalist premiss: without a territory of their own, the Jews could not become a proper 'people'—like English, French, Germans, Greeks, Italians, Irish, Poles, or Czechs. The Zionist idea was predicated on the Wilsonian principle of national self-determination. But Zionism also drew heavily on the eschatological ideas embedded in Jewish religious tradition. Redemption meant the physical return of Jews to the Land of Israel—a sacred territory promised to their Hebrew ancestor Abraham, by God. Redemption conveys both secular and religious meanings. Irredentism—the urge to restore 'unredeemed' land to the nation—was an important component of the nationalist movements, including fascism and Nazism—that emerged in Europe after the First World War. Non-religious Zionism shares with fascism the idea that a particular piece of territory belongs inalienably to one nation: in this respect there is no essential difference in kind between Zionist claims on Palestine and, say, the Italian irredentist claims on the port of Fiume on the Dalmatian coast, a part of the formerly Venetian territory awarded to Yugoslavia after the First World War. Yet even the secular right-wing Zionists known as 'revisionists' perceived Israel's expanding borders as stages on the road to redemption. Ian Lustick calls them, somewhat oxymoronically, the 'non-religious wing of the fundamentalist movement'. Led by Geula Cohen and Rafael Eitan, the revisionists see the religious Zionists' emphasis on the Land of Israel and its settlement as opportunity to enlist the support of religious Jews for maximalist nationalist aims. The Tehiya Party which Cohen led in the Knesset (parliament) supported the Gush Emunim settlements and forbade public desecration of the sabbath. As Cohen explained: 'All members of Tehiya believe that we are living at the beginning of Redemption even if no one knows its exact definition.'[6] By deliberately exploiting the eschatological expectations of the religious right, these secular right-wing Zionists acknowledge that religion is a more effective ideological basis for their expansionist aims than the strand of secular or 'romantic' nationalism they themselves represent.

Similarly the goal of *aliya,* the 'in-gathering' of the Jews from all over the world, exemplified in Israel's Law of Return (which automatically confers citizenship on anyone who can prove his or her Jewish descent), is both secular and religiously eschatological in character. The boundaries between the secular nationalist ideology of 'redemption' and a religious one are inextricably blurred.

Prior to the Holocaust, only a small section within orthodox European Jewry accepted Zionism. The key figure in the development of religious Zionism was the Latvian Rabbi Abraham Isaac Kook, who migrated to Palestine with his followers in 1919 and went on to create an orthodox stream of Zionism that combined the values of both movements. His son Rabbi Zvi Yehuda Kook founded the first political party of religious Zionists, the National Religious Party (NRP). In the 1960s he established a set of yeshiva seminaries in which orthodox Jews were allowed to combine their religious studies with military service. Immediately after the June 1967 war, in which Israel occupied East Jerusalem and the West Bank territory formerly controlled by Jordan, Rabbi Kook Jr stated: 'I tell you explicitly that the Torah [known by Christians as the Old Testament] forbids us to surrender even one inch of our liberated land. There are no conquests here and we are not occupying foreign lands; we are returning to our home, to the inheritance of our ancestors. There is no Arab land here, only the inheritance of our God.'[7]

Gush Emunim, the principal settler movement, was founded by members of the NRP in 1974. Its function was to bring about what was explicitly described as 'the redemption of the Land of Israel in our time'. This was to be achieved by allowing Jews to settle anywhere in the occupied territories, and by political campaigning. Gush Emunim members saw themselves as reviving ancient Israel. They named their settlements after ancient biblical towns and their children after Old Testament heroes. As their leader Rabbi Moshe Levinger put it, the land conquered in 1967 had been returned to its rightful owners as promised to their biblical ancestors by God. Gush Eminum deliberately breached Israeli government rules banning settlements near Arab towns. As one of their leaders, Rabbi Ben Nun, declared: 'Jewish immigration to Israel and settlement are beyond the law. The settlers' movement comes out of the Zionist constitution and no law can stop it ... For those to whom the Bible and the religious prescripts are beyond the law there is no need to say anything further.'[8] To the charge that they were acting in contravention to the will of the people expressed through their elected government another Gush Emunim rabbi replied: 'For us, what really matters is not democracy, but the Kingdom of Israel ... Democracy is a sacred idea for the Greeks, not so for the Jews.'[9]

The NRP has participated in every governing coalition since 1967. It supports the Jewish settlers and has encouraged annexation of the Occupied Territories. It voted against the 1998 Oslo Accords granting limited autonomy to the Palestinians. Its current chairman, the former Brigadier-General Effi Eitam, has spoken in favour of the 'transfer' of the Arab population (a euphemism for 'ethnic cleansing' or expulsion), a policy previously confined to fringe figures such as the late Rabbi Meir Kahane, who was prevented from standing for the Israeli parliament on account of his extremist views. As Israel's political centre of gravity has moved to the right, such views have become more commonplace and more respectable. One of Kahane's leading followers, Baruch Goldstein, an American-educated physician who opened fire in a Muslim prayer hall near the Tomb of the Patriarchs in Hebron in February 1994, killing at least 29 worshippers, including several children, has become a hero for the settlers. Not only was he not condemned by anyone in the settlers' movement, the Israeli government allowed his funeral cortège to pass through the streets of Jerusalem, before his burial in the settlement of Kiriat Arba. In his eulogy Rabbi Israel Ariel commended Goldstein as a 'holy martyr' who from now on would act as the settlers' 'intercessor in heaven. Goldstein did not act as an individual; he heard the cry of the land of Israel, which is being stolen from us day after day by the Muslims. He acted to relieve that cry of the Land ... The Jews will inherit the land not by any peace agreement, but only by shedding blood.'[10]

A poll conducted after the massacre revealed that at least 50 per cent of Israeli Jews would approve of it provided it was described, euphemistically, as a 'Patriarch's Cave Operation'—the term employed for the atrocity by Israeli settlers.[11] Goldstein's status as martyr is the mirror-image of the suicide bomber of Hamas or Islamic Jihad, whose act of terror is described as an act of 'self-martyrdom' (*istishhad*) within his (and, in several instances, her) community. Muslims who support the Palestinian suicide bombers see them as acting in the same spirit of martyrdom and self-sacrifice as the Jewish settlers and their supporters see Goldstein. In the same way the status of hero-martyr is conferred on Khalid Islambouli, executed for assassinating Anwar Sadat, the Egyptian president who signed the Camp David Peace Treaty with Israel, and Yigael Amir, assassin of the Israeli Prime Minister Yitzhak Rabin, who signed the Oslo Accords with PLO Chairman Yasser Arafat. According to Israeli authors Michael Karpin and Ina Friedman, Amir was a 'serious, deeply religious and thoroughly well-adjusted student' who made no secret of his view that Rabin was *din rodef*—the Halachic term for a traitor who endangers Jewish lives, and may therefore be killed as a measure of collective self-defence.[12] Islambouli's act was justified in a tract written by his mentor, Abd al-Salaam al-Farraj, who was also executed for his part in Sadat's killing. Entitled *The Neglected Duty* or *Missing Precept*—a reference to the doctrine of *jihad*—Farraj's tract drew heavily on the writings of Ibn Taymiyya (d. 1328), a religious scholar widely admired by the Islamists, who attacked the recently converted Mongul rulers of Syria for failing to rule in accordance with Islamic law.[13] Before he shot Rabin at point-blank range, Amir had ritually purified himself and obtained through an accomplice a rabbinical ruling to the effect that 'the moment a Jew turns over his people and land to enemies, he must be killed for endangering the lives of Jews'. Amir readily confessed to the killing, and is now serving a life sentence: he did not, however, reveal the name of the rabbis who ruled that his actions conformed to the Halakha.[14]

The religious Zionists of Gush Emunim who refuse to give back Arab territory and the Islamists of Hamas and Islamic Jihad who refuse any accommodation with Israel are in paradoxical collusion against secular-minded Jews and Palestinians in their opposition to any settlement involving a mutual accommodation between the contested territorial claims of Israel and Palestine. The old-style secular nationalists of the Palestine Liberation Organization (PLO) have met (in principle) the secular demands of Israel by accepting its right to exist as a Jewish state in accordance with United Nations resolutions. The Israelis for their part (with the greatest reluctance, in the case of the Sharon government) have given formal recognition to Palestinian rights by accepting the reality of the Palestine National Authority, while colluding with the settlers in limiting its power and undermining its authority. There exists a precarious basis for an accommodation but the religious rejectionists on both sides are making this difficult, if not impossible, by raising the ante, elevating the historic quarrel between Arabs and Israelis into a Manichaean struggle between the absolute values of good

BOX 20

The Land of Israel: A Gift from God

God promised the land of Israel to the Jews thousands of years ago. He won't let anyone take it away ... I want to show you the extent of the land because Solomon, the son of David who was living in 950 BC ... this was his territory. You go all the way up north to the Euphrates River which encompasses the better part of modern-day Syria. Solomon's empire went up to the Euphrates River ... This is Judea and Samaria and they are fighting in Jenin and Nablus. And Ramalla north of Jerusalem. And Bethlehem. And all of this is so called West Bank territory.

But that was just a small part of what God gave to them. And now, can Israel survive? Of course, it will survive because God is going to defend it. And why is America in favor of Israel? Because we have a great history of biblical belief—Judeo-Christian—and we believe God gave the land to the descendants of Israel. It was not given to Palestine, it wasn't given to so-called Palestinians. It wasn't given to Saudis or the Syrians. It was given to the descendants of Abraham, Isaac and Jacob through Joshua ... And God is not going to let anybody take it away from them.

(Pat Robertson's commentary (CBN, 5 June 2003) on President George W. Bush's announcement that America would support the 'Road Map' leading to a Palestinian State) and evil. The prospects for peace are further diminished by the support of Christian fundamentalists such as Pat Robertson for the extreme Zionist positions.

When conflicts are hyped in this way, violence is the inevitable concomitant. Religious nationalism further inflates nationalist rhetoric by giving it a cosmic dimension. Rabbi Kook the elder saw a universalist dimension in the foundation of Israel, not just salvation for the Jewish people: 'All the civilizations of the world will be renewed by the renaissance of our spirit. All quarrels will be resolved, and our revival will cause all life to be luminous with the joy of fresh birth.'[15] For Hamas and other Islamist organizations the struggle with Israel is transnational and cosmic. A communiqué issued after US troops were sent to Saudi Arabia in 1990 described it as 'another episode in the fight between good and evil' and 'a hateful Christian plot against our religion, our civilization and our land'.[16] In January 2003 President George W. Bush himself echoed the rhetoric of the Islamists like Bin Laden who see conflicts between Muslim and Western governments in terms of an age-long struggle between good Muslims and evil 'Jews and Crusaders', when he packaged Arab nationalist Iraq, Islamist Iran, and communist North Korea—three countries with utterly different ideologies and with few if any connections between them—into a monolithic 'axis of evil'.

The effect of such rhetoric is twofold. In societies such as America, Ireland, or parts of the Muslim world where religion has been an important part of the culture as well as an agent of socialization, the use of religious language has great mobilizing potential. People will respond positively to political messages couched in language associated with religion, because religion is thought of as 'good'. But the use of such language also tends to transcendentalize disputes, elevating them, as it were, from the mundane to the cosmic level. The result is that conflicts are absolutized, rendering them more intractable, less susceptible to negotiation. Where people acknowledge the realities of competing interests (as, for example, in the national bargaining sessions over agricultural quotas in the European Union) compromise is not only possible: it is the only game in town. Where religious language is invoked, as in Ireland or Israel-Palestine, the play of interests is transcendentalized, subsumed, as it were, into a much grander, Manichaean contest, between polarized opposites of absolute good versus evil. Since every nationalist group is likely to clash with the competing nationalisms of its neighbours, religious language intensifies conflict, because most nationalisms arise where identities are contested or where land is subject to competing claims. To be more precise, the use of religious language as a strategy for mobilizing support is most likely to succeed in situations where national or ethnic identities are grounded in religion or sustained by religious differences. In absolutizing the conflict, the play of competing interests—the stuff of normal politics—is forgotten or overruled.

The Israeli example is instructive. As members of a First World, industrial society accustomed to Western lifestyles with swimming pools, flush-toilets, and other modern conveniences, the Israeli settlers are greedy for water, a scarce resource in Palestine. According to recent accounts, Israeli settlers are now using 80 per cent of the water available to farmers in Palestine. When religious language is used, the illegal and disproportionate use of water is translated into a God-given grant of land and water-rights to Abraham. In the biblical rhetoric of the settlers, the Jews are God's special people; the Arab Palestinians are identified with the Amalekites, a Caananite tribe whom the ancient Hebrews were commanded to annihilate totally, with their women, children, and flocks.[17] Where good and evil, God and the Devil, are ranged in opposite camps, who would deliberately choose the latter? Far from being its ideological competitor, the religious 'fundamentalism' in Israel-Palestine, Chechnya, Kashmir, Sri Lanka, and many other of the world's most troubled regions is best understood as an intensification or deepening of nationalism by way of religion's mobilizing potential.

South Asian religious fundamentalisms provide a good illustration of this argument. If one looks at fundamentalism in terms of its primary Protestant meaning as defending the 'fundamentals' or orthodoxy of a religious tradition, there is a case for saying that the 'F-word' should not be applied to movements such as the RSS in India and its political offshoots, the BJP currently leading the governing coalition in Delhi, the VHP (Vishva Hindu Parishad, 'World Hindu Society'), the Sikh Akali Dal Party in the Punjab, and the Sinhalese nationalist party ruling in mainly Buddhist Sri Lanka.

The sociologist Steve Bruce produces three arguments for excluding these South Asian movements from his definition of fundamentalism. First, he says, with reference to the BJP and VHP, they have been 'provoked more by the threat of Islam than by a decline in religious observance by Hindus'. Second, they are directed more towards expelling or subordinating 'foreigners' (as they see most Muslims) than to revitalizing and purifying the Hindu faithful: 'there is no decline in orthodoxy to redress, because there is no orthodoxy.' Third, they are only tangentially a reaction to secularization. For these and other reasons Bruce concludes that 'the monotheistic religions of Judaism, Christianity and Islam offer much more fertile soil for fundamentalism than Hinduism and Buddhism.'[18]

On the face of it the three Abrahamic monotheisms might seem more susceptible to political exploitation of the kind we have been describing than Hindu polytheism or Buddhism, because of the absence in these traditions of an orthodoxy based on a single scriptural tradition. As Bruce argues, 'Hinduism might be better described not as a religion but as a loose collection of religions—that of the Shaivites, the Vaishnavas, the Shaktas, the Smartas and others—that share some common themes but that tolerate a huge variety of expressions of those themes.'[19] Unlike the Abrahamic traditions, each of which has a canonical scripture that can function as a rallying point for defence, the Hindu tradition contains such an abundance of scriptures, laws, and philosophies that 'it becomes very difficult to single out any one specific item' as being basic or 'fundamental'.[20]

Despite this important difference, however, there are compelling parallels that Bruce overlooks. Like its Islamic counterpart, Hindu revivalism with its nationalist or fundamentalist offshoots is rooted in a reformist religious tradition more than a century old. The original movement was not in the first instance anti-Muslim but anti-colonial, stimulated by the British administration's pigeonholing of India's religious communities into identifiable and hence manageable groups according to the principle of 'divide and rule'. From the 1871 census the British defined their Indian subjects according to religion. With the intro-duction of democratic institutions at local level, starting in 1909, religious groupings were organized into separate electorates, with a number of constituencies reserved for Muslims in each province, and similar arrangements for Christians in Madras and Sikhs in the Punjab. For the educated Hindu elite the need to cultivate their own con-stituencies meant 'delineating a broad-based communal identity' beyond the old caste system. The creation of a new 'Hindu' identity inevitably generated reciprocal responses amongst Muslims and Sikhs (as well as from the smaller

Jain and Parsee communities whose separate identities were acknowledged), with all of the three main groups competing against each other for a 'privileged position in colonial society'.[21]

The reformist movements within 'Hinduism' (a term invented by Europeans) bear some 'family resemblances' to the Islamic *salafi* movement that originated in colonial Egypt towards the end of the nineteenth century. Swami Dayananda Sarasvati (1824–83), founder of Arya Samaj—the Society of Aryas—is one of the spiritual and intellectual progenitors of the RSS and its offshoot the BJP. In some respects he resembles Afghani in his rejection of tradition and the search he undertook for a modernized, more rational religion that would regenerate his society. A Brahman from a well-to-do Shaivite family in Gujarat, he was profoundly affected, aged 14, by watching a mouse consume (and pollute) offerings of food made to the statue of Shiva during an all-night vigil when other members of his family had dozed off. According to his autobiography Dayananda felt it impossible 'to reconcile the idea of an omnipotent, living god with this idol which allows the mice to run over his body and thus suffers his image to be polluted without the slightest protest'. After wandering around India for thirteen years as a holy man (a conventional apprenticeship for an aspiring guru) Dayananda found a teacher who persuaded him to preach his reformist doctrines in Hindi (the popular vernacular) rather than in learned Sanskrit.

Some of Dayananda's ideas reveal an affinity with the 'fundamentalisms' to be found in the Abrahamic traditions. He believed that the Indian scriptures—the Vedas—were the highest revelations ever vouchsafed to humanity, and contained all knowledge, scientific as well as spiritual. 'All the knowledge that is extant in the world' he would claim 'originated in Aryavarta'—the Land of Arya, his name for ancient India, a mythical realm whose kings ruled over all the earth and taught wisdom to all their peoples. Through their vast knowledge the ancient Indians were able to produce the weapons of war described in the great epics such as the Mahabharata. 'Since the knowledge of the Vedas is of general applicability, all references to kings and battles are in fact political or military directives.'[22] The sentiment is identical to that of the Islamists who recall the age of the 'Rightly Guided Caliphs' as an era of justice and prosperity (although in actual fact, three of the first four caliphs were brutally murdered). His point about military directives is strikingly similar to an argument employed by the Islamist writer Sayyid Qutb in *Milestones*, the tract he wrote while in prison in Egypt before his execution in 1966. Muhammad's Companions, according to Qutb, used the Koran not just for aesthetic or even moral guidance, but as a manual for action 'as a soldier on the battlefield' reads his daily bulletin.[23]

Dayananda's ideas first took root among Hindus in the Punjab, which has large Muslim and Sikh populations, and it was Punjabi leaders of the Arya Samaj who founded

organized into groups that transcend or substitute for family ties. Hasan al-Banna, founder of the Muslim Brotherhood, grouped his followers into 'families and battalions'; young Palestinians who today volunteer for suicide missions are organized into 'friendship packs' who may act as family substitutes, while holding them to their decision.[25] The organizers of the RSS model themselves on Hindu renunciates. 'Dedicated to a higher goal [they] are supposed to abandon family ties and material wealth.' Like the Palestinian and Lebanese volunteers belonging to the Shia Hezbollah, they are generally young, unmarried men in their twenties. They wear Indian-style dress and are expected to lead an exemplary, ascetic existence, although some may marry and have families after a period of service. Organizers serve without salary, but their material needs are taken care of. Some volunteers are provided with motor scooters for getting around town. Both the Brotherhood and the RSS consciously blend elements of modernity with aspects of tradition. Al-Banna sought to infuse his organization with some of the spiritual values of Sufism (Islamic mysticism) without its devotional excesses. As leader he called himself the *murshid*, or guide, a title usually reserved for the leaders of Sufi orders; his favourite reading, al-Ghazali's *Revitalization of the religious sciences*, is strongly informed by Sufi mysticism. In a similar manner the RSS leaders blended the prestige of secular learning with spiritual knowledge. The founder K. B. Hedgewar who ran the organization from 1925 to 1940 was known to his followers by the honorific *Doctorji*. His successor, M. S. Golwalkar (1940–73), was called *Guruji*. Both the Muslim Brotherhood and the RSS blended indigenous ideas of spiritual leadership with organizational techniques borrowed from Western bureaucracy.[26]

The Hindu movement's leading intellectual was V. D. Savarkar (1883–1966), who held the presidency of the Hindu Mahasabha from 1937 to 1942. Like Sayyid Qutb he wrote his most influential work, *Hindutva*, 'Hindu-ness', in prison, where he spent many years after his detention by the British in 1910. *Hindutva* is a manifesto for religious nationalism. As Daniel Gold explains, Savarkar's 'idea of Hindu Nation stands in contrast to the idea of a composite, territorially defined political entity that developed among the secular nationalists and would be enshrined in the Indian constitution. The modern western idea of nation, according to Savarkar, does not do justice to the ancient glory of the Hindu people, the indigenous and numerically dominant population of the subcontinent. The people whose culture grew up and developed in greater India— from the Himalayas to the southern seas, by some accounts from Iran to Singapore—this, for Savarkar was the Hindu Nation. The subcontinent is their motherland, and Hinduness is the quality of their national culture.'[27] *Hindutva* is not the same as Hindu religious orthodoxy because, according to Savarkar, its spirit is manifest in other South Asian religions, including Jainism, Sikhism, and Indian Buddhism. Muslims and Christians, by contrast, are seen as foreign elements in the subcontinent, which rightly belongs to Hindus. 'Hindus should actively reject any alien dominance: they have done so in the past and should renew their struggle valiantly whenever necessary.' For Savarkar India is both 'Fatherland' and 'Holyland': as Gold points out, this definition deliberately excludes Muslims and Christians for whom India is not a holy land. 'From the viewpoint of Hindu cultural nationalism, Savarkar's formulation effectively isolates the perceived other.'[28]

Golwalkar, like his Indian contemporary, the Islamist ideologue Mawdudi, expressed his admiration for the Nazis in Germany, who held similar ideas about national purity. 'Germany has shocked the world by purging the country of the semitic races—the Jews,' he wrote in 1939 before the full horror of Nazi atrocities had taken place. 'Race pride at its highest has been manifested here. Germany has also shown how well-nigh impossible it is for Races [sic] and cultures, having differences going to the root, to be assimilated into one united whole, a good lesson for us in Hindusthan to learn and profit by.'[29]

As suggested above, there is a 'fundamentalistic' element in Dayananda's elevation of the Vedas to the *summum* of human knowledge along with his myth of the golden age of Aryavartic kings. But the predominant tone, and its consequences, are nationalist. *Hindutva* secularizes Hinduism by sacralizing the nation, bringing the cosmic whole within the realm of human organization. As Gold astutely observes, 'If personal religion entails among other things the identification of the individual with some larger whole, then the Hindu Nation may appear as a whole more immediately visible and attainable than the ritual cosmos of traditional Hinduism.'[30] The problem, of course, is that such a sacralization of nationality is explicitly anti-pluralistic. Both Arya Samaj and the RSS define their religion in contradistinction to other groups. The 'Hindu-ization' of Indian nationalism generated a reciprocal response among Muslims that led to the traumatic par-tition of the subcontinent in 1947, with many thousands killed or maimed in communal rioting. The shock of the sainted Mahatma Gandhi's assassination by an RSS mem-ber in January 1948 allowed Nehru to ban the RSS and its affiliates, enabling Congress to foist upon India a secular Constitution that lies 'squarely in the best Western tradition'.[31] As Sunil Khilnani observes, 'Constitutional democracy based on universal suffrage did not emerge from popular pressures for it within Indian society, it was not wrested by the people from the state; it was given to them by the political choice of an intellectual élite.'[32]

The sacralization of Indian identity would remain a potent, corrosive force in the body politic, a sleeping giant that could all too easily be woken by politicians willing to play the communal card. Job reservations or affirmative action programmes aimed at protecting 'scheduled castes' (the former Untouchables), could be presented as clashing with the rights or aspirations of the majority. In the words of a former state director-general of police and official of the VHP affiliated to the RSS: 'We feel that what we are doing is good for the country. After all what is good for 82 per cent of the country is good for the rest of the country, isn't it?'[33] The 'Fundamental Rights' guaranteeing 'freedom of conscience and free profession, practice and propagation or religion' under article 25 of the Constitution would remain highly problematic in a society as religious as India's. As T. N. Madan points out, 'secularism does not mean in India that religion is privatized: such an idea is alien to the indigenous religious traditions, which are holistic in character and do not recognize such dualistic categories as sacred versus profane, religious versus secular, or public versus private.'[34]

One of the severest tests facing India's secular constitutional arrangements has come from the 'fundamentalist', or rather nationalist, movement within the minority Sikh community. Space does not allow an adequate description of Sikh fundamentalism. However T. N. Madan's account in *Fundamentalisms Observed* makes it abundantly clear that the Sikh movement led by the charismatic preacher Jarnail Singh Bhindranwale (1947–84) fits the pattern of movements in other religious traditions that have turned to, or ended in, violence. A relatively young religion founded in the Punjab during the sixteenth century, Sikhism constantly faced the possibility of being reabsorbed into the Hindu mainstream from which it originally sprang. Its distinctive identity was buttressed by the

others as human shields, while permitting his followers to desecrate it.[36] There are parallels here with the seizure of the sanctuary in Mecca, Islam's holiest shrine, by the Saudi rebel Juhaiman al-Utaibi in November 1979. Operation Blue Star, the Indian Army's attack on the Golden Temple in June 1984, resulted in more than a thousand deaths (including Bhindranwale's), many of them innocent pilgrims. Shortly afterwards Prime Minister Indira Gandhi, who authorized the attack, was murdered by her trusted Sikh bodyguards. Nearly three thousand Sikhs lost their lives in the ensuing rioting in Delhi and other cities. In a retaliatory attack, Sikh terrorists may have been responsible for the crash of an Air India jumbo jet off the Irish coast in June 1985, killing all 329 people on board.[37]

The second major challenge to India's secular constitution took place seven years later, in 1992, when a gang of Hindu militants destroyed the Babri Masjid (mosque of Babur) in the town of Ayodhya, south-east of Delhi. Ayodhya is the mythical birthplace of Lord Rama, hero of the Rayama, one of the great Indian epics, and an incarnation of the great god Vishnu. The Kingdom of Ayodhya over which Rama rules with his beautiful consort Sita after his exile and travails in the forest, epitomizes the golden age of Aryavarta as described by Dayananda. Rama's alleged birthplace, however, became the site of a mosque said to have been constructed on the orders of Babur, the first Moghul emperor, after a visit to the city in 1528. In 1949, two years after Independence, local worshippers reported the miraculous appearance of Rama's image in the building. (Muslims, more sceptically, believed it had been put there by local Hindu activists.) An outbreak of communal rioting persuaded the local magistrate to close the building—but he allowed Hindu worshippers to visit it once a year on the anniversary of the image's appearance. The build-up to the crisis started in earnest in 1986 when a local court allowed the building to be opened for Hindu worship. In the ensuing riots bombs were set off, shops were burned, and at least twenty people died. By 1989 the confrontation had became a major national issue, with an all-India campaign by Hindu activists to construct a new temple at the site. Small donations were sought from millions of ordinary people; villagers from all over India collaborated in making bricks for the temple's construction. Tensions escalated throughout the summer, with increasing communal rioting taking place as the elections approached. The government's efforts at mediation were unsuccessful, and in November the Congress faction led by Indira's son Rajiv Gandhi was defeated at the polls. His successor proved no more successful at defusing the tension. In December 1992, in defiance of the courts and their own religious leaders, a group of Hindu hotheads demolished the mosque during a ceremony for the dedication of the new temple, many of them using their bare hands. In an action that infuriated India's Muslims (and would have wide repercussions in Pakistan) the 13,000 police and militiamen who had been drafted to protect the site failed to intervene. The subsequent riots in Bombay and other cities were the worst since India's independence in 1947. In a series of pogroms thousands of innocent Muslims lost their lives: even in Bombay's affluent Colobar district where real estate prices rival those of Tokyo and New York, middle-class Muslims found it necessary to remove their names from lists of residents on apartment blocks, fearing lynching by the mob.[38]

Sri Lanka provides a further example of South Asian religious nationalism. Here, in a situation that bears a certain resemblance to Ireland, the demand for recognition of its separate status by an island minority linked by religion and ethnicity to its larger neighbour (in this case Hindu Tamils of southern India) is perceived by members of the majority community—Sinhalese Buddhists—as a threat to the nation's integrity. Like Irish Catholicism the Theravada Buddhism of Sri Lanka has developed into a nationalist ideology in which religion has become a marker of communal identity. The reasons are largely historical. Sri Lankan Buddhists regard themselves as the survivors of the great Buddhist empire founded in India by King Asoka in the third century BCE. While in mainland India Buddhism eventually disappeared as society relapsed into the multiform patterns of worship which came to be known as Hinduism, the Sinhalese held to the Buddhist faith which eventually became politicized. In Sri Lanka (as in Burma), Buddhism provided the stirrings of anti-colonial sentiment by offering 'the only universally acceptable

symbol to represent an accumulation of grievances, economic, social and psychological, which were as yet, for the
most part, inarticulate and incapable of direct political
exploitation'.[39] A reformist movement among the laity—
stimulated in part by the American theosophist Colonel
Olcott—won some concessions from the British but in
general the colonial authorities were hostile towards the
Buddhist sangha (religious institution), which they saw as
a threat to their power. The most articulate spokesman
of the new 'reformed' or nationalist Buddhism came to
be known as the Anagarika Dharmapala (the Homeless
Guardian of the Dharma or universal law). An Afghani-like
figure who occupied a position somewhere between a
monk and a lay politician, he formulated, according to
Donald Swearer, a 'simplified, moralistic Buddhist ideology' that was doubtless stimulated by the challenge
posed by Protestant missionaries. Like Hasan al-Banna,
Dharmapala fulminated against the social vices deemed
to have been introduced under colonial auspices, while
harking back to an early, heroic age when righteousness
prevailed—in this case the reign of King Dutthagamani
(161–137 BCE), who wrested control from a Tamil ruler
and thus became an exemplary nationalist hero: 'My
message to the young men of Sri Lanka is ... Believe not
the alien who is giving you arrack, whisky, toddy, saus-
ages, who makes you buy his goods at clearance sales ...
Enter into the realm of our King Dutthagamani in spirit
and try to identify ourself with the thoughts of the great

king who rescued Buddhism and our nationalism from oblivion.'[40]

In 1956, the year of Britain's Suez debacle, S. W. R. D. Bandaranaike, leader of the opposition Sri Lankan Freedom Party (SLFP), was able to win power on a pro-Buddhist, pro-Sinhalese ticket, replacing the upper-class, English-educated liberals of the United National Party who had governed the country since independence. The SLFP benefited hugely from celebration of the 2500th anniversary of the Buddha's birth (Buddha Jayanti) the following year and from the previous publication of a report detailing the suppression of Buddhism under the British. The Jayanti enlarged upon and celebrated the national myth bonding the Buddhist faith to the land and the Sinhalese nation which 'had come into being with the blessing of the Buddha as a "chosen race" with a divine mission to fulfil, and now stands on the threshold of a new era leading to its "great destiny"'.[41] The SLFP was aggressively supported by the United Monks' Front, which rejected the concept of secular nationhood in terms very similar to those that would be used by Ayatollah Khomeini in his famous Najaf lectures.

The 'Buddhisization' of Sri Lankan politics had the inevitable consequence of making non-Buddhists (Tamils and Muslims) feel excluded from the nation, provoking demands by Tamil separatists for a state of their own. The Tamil Tigers—as the activists called themselves—were concerned not only with securing political rights, but more

BOX 21

In ancient days, according to the records of history, the welfare of the nation and the welfare of the religion were regarded as synonymous terms by the laity as well as by the Sangha. The divorce of religion from the nation was an idea introduced into the minds of the Sinhalese by invaders from the West who belonged to an alien faith. It was a convenient instrument of astute policy to enable them to keep the people in subjugation in order to rule the people as they pleased.

It was in their own interests and not for the welfare of the people that these foreign invaders attempted to create a gulf between the bhikkus (monks) and the laity—a policy which they implemented with diplomatic cunning. We should not follow their example and should not attempt to withdraw the bhikkus from society. Such conduct would assuredly be a deplorable act of injustice, committed against our nation, our country, our religion.

(Statement by The United Monks' Front, 1946, in Donald K. Swearer,
'Fundamentalist Movements in Theravada Buddhism',
in Marty and Appleby, *Fundamentalism Observed*)

importantly with maintaining a cultural, ethnic, and religious identity which had been suppressed or alienated as Sinhalese nationalism became increasingly reliant on Buddhist symbols. More than 60,000 people from both communities lost their lives in the ensuing civil war that lasted nearly two decades. In the late 1980s the Tigers resorted increasingly to the novel tactic—pioneered by the

Shii Hezbollah in Lebanon—of suicide bombing. More often than not the victims were civilians. A steady campaign of assassinations (including that of the Indian Prime Minister, Rajiv Gandhi, in 1991, by a female bomber) and indiscriminate murder was kept up through the 1990s. In 1996, 91 people died, and 1,400 were wounded, in the suicide bombing of Colombo's Central Bank; 18 were killed in the destruction of the twin-towered World Trade Centre in Colombo in 1997; 16 died in the suicidal attack on a Buddhist shrine in Kandy in 1998. Some, though not all, the Tigers were practising Hindus, who dedicated themselves to Shiva before sacrificing themselves—and others.

The example of Buddhism in Sri Lanka clearly demonstrates that none of the major religious traditions is immune from 'fundamentalism', to which violence is closely linked—though it might be better in this, as in most other contexts, to describe the process as the 'nationalization' or secularization of religion. Donald Swearer argues that by 'homogenizing' the Buddhist tradition and reducing it to a simplified core teaching along with a moralistic programme of right living linked to Sinhalese Buddhist identity, Bandaranaike (and his later successor President Jayawardine) 'ignored the polar dynamic between the transmundane and the mundane, a distinction basic not only to traditional Theravada Buddhism but to the other great historical religions as well. The absolutism of fundamentalism stems from this basic transformation of the religious worldview.' The narrowly ideological nature of 'fundamentalism', Swearer concludes, means that it is 'not religious in the classical sense of that term but rather a variant of a secular faith couched in religious language'. In this process traditional religious symbols are 'stripped of their symbolic power to evoke a multiplicity of meanings'. Like Juergensmeyer, Swearer sees nationalism as triumphing over religion, rather than the reverse: 'Religions thus harnessed to nationalism are often regarded as more pure and orthodox than the traditional forms they seek to supplant; in turn nationalism readily takes on the character of a fervid, absolutistic revival of religion. In the case of Sri Lanka, as elsewhere, the search for national identity is prior and conditions the fundamentalism of the religion(s) incorporated into nationalism.'[42]

The heart of the fundamentalist project, in line with this analysis, lies not in religion but in the essentially modern agenda of extending or consolidating the power of the national state—or, to use the term preferred by the Israeli sociologist S. N. Eisenstadt, the revolutionary 'Jacobin' state that appeared with the French Revolution and the movements that surfaced in its wake, including communism and fascism (though he tactfully avoids mentioning Zionism). According to Eisenstadt, the fundamentalists appropriated some of the 'central aspects of the political program of modernity', including its 'participatory, totalistic and egalitarian orientations' while rejecting the Enlightenment values embedded in Jacobinism, including the sovereignty and autonomy of reason and the perfectibility of man.[43]

'The basic structure or phenomenology of their vision and action', he concludes, 'is in many crucial and seemingly paradoxical ways a modern one, just as was the case with the totalitarian movements of the twenties and thirties. ... These movements bear within themselves the seeds of very intensive and virulent revolutionary sectarian, utopian Jacobinism, seeds which can, under appropriate circumstances, come to full-blown fruition.'[44] Such movements have always had violent repercussions: before developing its modern meaning of freelance or irregular military action, the word 'terrorist' was applied to the Jacobin revolutionaries in France who used the power of the state to inflict terror on their enemies.

The use of violence, whether by revolutionaries who seize control of the state, or by freelancers who challenge the government, is neither arbitrary nor meaningless. Studies of religious conflicts in Europe and South Asia reveal similar patterns of violence. Examining religious riots in sixteenth-century France, Natalie Zemon Davis discovered 'rites of violence' that bore many of the hallmarks of religious activity. 'Even extreme ways of defiling corpses—dragging bodies through the streets and throwing them to the dogs, dismembering genitalia and selling them in mock commerce—and desecrating religious objects' had 'perverse connections' with such religious concepts as 'pollution and purification, heresy and blasphemy'.[45] In his analysis of religious violence in South Asia Stanley Tambiah reaches similar conclusions. For example, in cases where innocent bystanders were burned alive by the crowd, the defenceless and terrified victims were murdered ritualistically in 'mock imitation of both the self-immolation of [Buddhist] conscientious objectors and the terminal rite of cremation'.[46]

If there is a common theme to the foregoing, as well as to the many more instances that must remain unmentioned, it may be found in the way that religion has become secularized in many parts of the world, even among people who claim to be resisting secularism. The mythical images of cosmic struggle which form part of the religious repertoire of the great traditions are being actualized or brought down to earth. 'The cosmic struggle is understood to be occurring in this world rather than in a mythical setting. Believers identify personally with the struggle.'[47] All religions affirm the primacy of meaning and order over chaos; hence in treating of death and violence, religions strive to contain them within an overarching, benign cosmic frame. In the Baghavad Gita the god Krishna tells the warrior Arjuna that he must submit to his destiny in fighting against his own kinsmen. In so doing, he assents to the disorder of the world, although the contestants know that in the grander sense, 'this disorder is corrected by a cosmic order that is beyond killing and being killed'.[48]

Similarly the Koran contains many allusions to the

Prophet Muhammad's battles, which are set in the wider context of a moral order deemed to be upheld by an all-seeing benevolent God. For Christians, Jesus's heroism in allowing himself to endure an excruciatingly painful death is seen as 'a monumental act of redemption for humankind, tipping the balance of power and allowing the struggle for order to succeed'.[49]

Religious images and texts provide ways in which violence, pain, and death are overcome symbolically. Human suffering is made more durable by the idea that death and pain are not pointless, that lives are not wasted needlessly, but are part of a grander scheme in which divinely constituted order reigns supreme above the chaos and disorder of the world. In such a context the horrors and chaos of wars, as described in the Mahabharata and the Book of Joshua, as debated in the Baghavad Gita, as predicted in the Book of Revelation, and as alluded to in the Koran, are subsumed within an order seen to be meaningful and ultimately benign. The reading and recitation of such texts, like the performance of ancient Greek tragedies, doubtless had a carthartic function, purging people of anger and rage, inducing pity and fear, reducing actual conflict, upholding social harmony. By its rejection of symbolic interpretations fundamentalism (at least in its politically militant versions) releases the violence contained in the text. Fundamentalism is religion materialized, the word made flesh, as it were, with the flesh rendered, all too often, into shattered body parts by the forces of holy rage.

Why is this happening in the twenty-first century? Why, when modernization seemed to have made the God of Battles redundant, if not dead, has religious violence resurfaced like Dracula, from the grave?

7

CONCLUSION

Until the mid-1970s it was widely assumed that politics was breaking away from religion and that as societies became more industrialized religious belief and practice would be restricted to private thoughts and activities. The decline in the social and political importance of religion in the West was grounded in the social scientific traditions flowing from the commanding figures of Karl Marx, Émile Durkheim, and Max Weber, all of whom insisted in different ways that secularization was integral to modernization. The processes of modern industrialism which Weber saw as being characterized by depersonalized functional relationships and increasing bureaucratization were leading, if not to the final 'death of God', at the least to the 'disenchantment of the world'. The numinous forces that had underpinned the medieval cosmos would be psychologized, subjectivized, and demythologized. On the face of it, the 1979 revolution in Iran seriously dented conventional wisdom. Here was a revolt deploying a repertoire of religious symbols that brought down a modernizing government and placed political power in the hands of a religious establishment steeped in medieval theology and jurisprudence. Moreover this was clearly an urban, not a rural, phenomenon—a response, perhaps, to 'over-rapid' or 'uneven' development, but not in any sense a movement such as the counter-revolutionary movements in the Vendée or the peasant jacqueries that challenged the secular project of the French Revolution.

Some commentators (myself included) argued that the

mix of politics and religion that came to fruition in Iran was peculiarly Islamic, or even uniquely Shii. Islam, it was said, unlike Christianity, had a built-in political agenda: the Prophet Muhammad had combined the role of revelator with that of state-builder, and that all who sought to follow his path must sooner or later be drawn into the political game. Shiism was a counter-cultural variation on this theme. Originally a protest movement against the worldly Umayyads who took over Muhammad's empire, it developed into a tradition of radical dissent, one that oscillated over the centuries between quietism and activism, withdrawal and revolt. The Khomeinist revolution—like the rise of the Shii Hezbollah in Lebanon—represented the swing of the Shii pendulum towards activism, after decades of sullen acquiescence in 'unrighteous' government.

By the early 1980s, however, it was becoming clear that religious activism was very far from being confined to the Islamic world and that newly politicized movements were occurring in virtually every major religious tradition. In America the New Christian Right (NCR) challenged and temporarily checked the boundaries of church–state separation that had steadily been moving in a secular direction. Commenting on the growth of evangelical and fundamentalist churches in America at the expense of the liberal 'mainstream', Peter Berger, doyen of Weberian sociologists, was forced to admit that 'serious intellectual difficulties' had been created 'for those (like myself) who thought that modernization and secularization were inexorably linked phenomena'.[1] Brushing aside the Muslim world, Berger suggested a theory of American exceptionalism. Like India, the USA was somehow irredeemably religious. Secularism of the sanitized, Scandinavian type was confined to university campuses and other privileged cultural enclaves. When it came to religion America was 'an India, with a little Sweden superimposed'.[2]

A theory of secularization that excludes America (the world's most advanced industrial society) and India (one of the world's most rapidly industrializing regions) as well as the Muslim world from its purview faces—to put it mildly—some major problems. One need hardly add that the collapse of communism in Eastern Europe has seen a marked resurgence in public religiosity, while Latin America and parts of Africa appear to be undergoing far-reaching religious transformations, with Pentecostalism overtaking Catholicism as the dominant religious tradition. With Japan and South Korea—Asia's most advanced industrial economies—ranking high in the list of countries nurturing new religious movements, only secular Western Europe and Australasia—areas that Martin Marty, the American historian of religion, calls 'the spiritual ice-belt'—appear to be conforming to the demise of the public deity so confidently pronounced by the founding fathers of modern social science.

Various theories have been advanced to explain the persistence or recent revival of religion, of which the 'fundamentalisms' we have been examining are an integral part. The two previous chapters explored the close connections between religious revival movements and nationalism. Where religion—or in certain cases religious difference— is a vital component in the construction of national identity or where religious feelings have been invoked in the course of the struggle against colonialism, as in many Third World countries, religious rhetoric retains its ability to mobilize and motivate. Thus without abandoning the secularization thesis altogether, Jeff Haynes suggests that secularization continues to make 'sustained progress' except when religion finds or retains work to do other than its pre-modern function of 'relating individuals to the supernatural'.[3] Haynes relates this paradoxically to the post-modern rejection of 'meta-narratives' or 'absolute ways of speaking truth'.

Postmodernism is an enigmatic concept, whose very ambiguity reflects the confusion and uncertainty inherent in contemporary life. The term is applied in and to many diverse spheres of human life and activity. It is important for politics as it decisively reflects the end of belief in the Enlightenment project, the assumption of universal progress based on reason, and in the modern Promethean myth of humanity's mastery of its destiny and capacity for resolution of all its problems.[4]

The relationship between fundamentalism and post-modernism is paradoxical because far from rejecting 'absolute ways of speaking truth', fundamentalisms exemplify them. The compliment post-modernism pays to religion is back-handed and treacherous. By proclaiming the end of positivism and the ideology of progress, which was supposed to have replaced or overtaken religion, post-modernism opens up public space for religion—but at the price of relativizing its claims to absolute truth. By saying, in effect, 'Your story is as good as mine, or his, or hers', post-modernism allows religious voices to have their say while denying their right to silence others, as religions have tended to do throughout history. For the true fundamentalist, the 'post-' prefixed to modernism is a catch, perhaps even a fraud, because modernity, in Anthony Gidden's formulation, is founded on the 'institutionalisation of doubt'. Far from 'de-institutionalizing' doubt, however, the pluralism implicit in a post-modernist outlook sanctifies it by opening the doors of choice, which is the enemy of certainty.

Theologically, fundamentalists must reject choice because they know there is only one truth that has been revealed to them by the 'supraempirical spiritual entity' most of them call God. But the contemporary situation under which this deity (or in some cases deities) makes demands on them are utterly different from those that prevailed in pre-modern times when most people were exposed to a single religious tradition within a cultural milieu largely formed by that tradition. The situation facing Muslims living in the West illustrates dilemmas that can be applied, with suitable modifications, to be-

Under modern conditions an open question—what is the proper way to behave?—is replaced by a much narrower one: how should Muslims (or followers of other faith traditions) behave under modern conditions?—the implication being that for Muslims nowadays the whole world has become *dar al-harb* because even in Muslim majority areas ways of living differently from the 'straight path' prescribed by Islam are ever-present alternatives. In pre-colonial times, during the era of what might be called the classical Islamic hegemony, the possibility of alternative non-Islamic lifestyles simply did not arise for the majority of people. Where pork is not available, no one has to make a decision about whether to eat hot-dogs. Where wine was the preserve of a privileged elite who drank it in the privacy of their palaces, the permissibility of alcohol consumption was not a burning social question. In a 'homosocial' society where women were strictly segregated, lesbian and gay relationships (though formally prohibited) were rarely seen as threatening to the social order. Under pressures from outside forces all these issues, especially those involving sexual appearance and behaviour, have acquired iconic significance as marking boundaries between the insiders and outsiders, the community of salvation and the 'unsaved' people who live beyond its boundaries. Thus in an archetypically Western milieu such as the American high school, Muslim identity defaults to gender segregation, with veiled Muslim coeds holding all-female 'proms' in order to avoid breaking the taboo on sexual mixing.⁵ Their evangelical Christian counterparts hold assemblies of 'promise-keepers', who proclaim their commitment to chastity before marriage and fidelity afterwards. In a pluralistic environment such as America, all religious groups will use behavioural restrictions as a way of marking the boundaries between believers and nonbelievers, between 'us' (the saved) and 'them' (the damned). Mormons abstain from tea and coffee as well as alcohol— so they are distinguishable from orthodox evangelicals who are mostly teetotal. Jehova's Witnesses avoid blood transfusions (and military service), Christian Scientists avoid conventional medicine (because Christ is the only Healer), and some Hasidic Jews (like some ultra-orthodox Muslims) exhibit behaviour bordering on incivility by refusing to shake hands with non-believers. Such behaviour is often described by those whom it is designed to exclude as 'fundamentalist'. One of the 'family resemblances' exhibited by movements in this book is the concern or even obsession with the drawing of boundaries that will set the group apart from the wider society by deliberately choosing beliefs or modes of behaviour which proclaim who they are and how they would like to be seen.

In this respect fundamentalisms are distinctly modern phenomena: like the New Religious Movements that have sprouted in some of the ₁nost industrialized parts of the world (notably South-East Asia and North America) they feed on contemporary alienation or anomie by offering solutions to contemporary dilemmas, buttressing the loss of identities sustained by many people (especially young people) at times of rapid social change, high social and geographic mobility, and other stress-inducing factors. As two well-known American observers put it: 'Fundamentalism is a truly modern phenomenon—modern in the sense that the movement is always seeking original solutions to new, pressing problems. Leaders are not merely constructing more rigid orthodoxies in the name of defending old mythical orthodoxies. In the process of undertaking "restoration" within contemporary demographic/technological centers, *new* social orders are actually being promulgated.'[6] The born-again Christian finds comfort and support, not just by internalizing the iconic figure of Jesus as a personal super-ego, but also by accessing the support of fellow believers. Islamist organizations such as Hamas are not just involved in armed resistance to the Israeli occupation of their land but dispose of a considerable range of welfare activities. As well as being places of worship, churches, mosques, and synagogues are the focus of social networks. The intensive religiosity exhibited by fundamentalists in all traditions may strengthen the support and increase the social opportunities the individual receives from such networks, though there are perils here as well: in the absence of disciplined hierarchies disputes about the interpretation of texts makes fundamentalists vulnerable to the splits that afflict many radical movements.

Fundamentalisms differ from 'cults' or New Religious Movements by their commitment to textual scripturalism. For example, the focus of the Rajneesh community in Oregon and Poona was on the person of Baghwan Shree Rajneesh, a charismatic 'cult' leader who drew eclectically on a wide variety of sources from Hinduism, Buddhism, Christian, and Islamic mysticism, psychoanalysis, and psychotherapy, as well as personal spiritual experience, in his teachings. A Christian fundamentalist such as Jerry Falwell, by contrast, sticks closely to the 'inerrant' text of the Bible in his sermons. This distinction, however, should not be drawn too sharply. David Koresh, the 'prophet' of the Branch Davidian sect of Seventh Day Adventism who perished along with dozens of his followers at Waco Texas in April 1993, when his compound was attacked by US federal agents, was a 'textual fundamentalist' as well as a charismatic leader who availed himself of the sexual services of his female followers in order to 'spread his seed'. Far from being the result of 'brain-washing' or 'mind-control' techniques, the charismatic power he exercised over his followers was the result of their conviction that he was a divinely inspired interpreter of biblical passages (particularly the Book of Revelation) that are central to the Seventh Day Adventist tradition. During the prolonged negotiations preceding the federal attack on the Waco compound after a 51-day siege, the FBI negotiators dismissed Koresh's sermonizing as mere 'Bible babble'. To his followers, however, his discourses on

America. By means of television, 'televangelists' such as Pat Robertson seek to challenge the secular order, by 're-enchanting' the world with divine interventions and supernatural events. Robertson and the late Oral Roberts have performed healings on camera, even claiming to heal viewers through their sets. In such programmes the sacred is reaffirmed, after being banished from secular networks, or at best restricted to the realm of fiction. The process of modernization described by Weber in his famous phrase 'the disenchantment of the world' is reversed. Through television the world is re-enchanted and resacralized.

At the same time the counter-attack on secular values mounted through religious television may prove subject to the law of diminishing returns. Through television the sacred and supernatural are domesticated, and ultimately banalized. In the end, disenchantment continues under the guise of the new religiosity. In the studio the charismatic leader who speaks for God must put himself under the control of the director and camera crew. Sacred words may disappear on the cutting-room floor. The structure of authority becomes ambiguous.

Television, mixing fact and fiction within a common format, collapses *mythos* and *logos*, especially in cultures where the conventions of theatre and fiction have recently been imported. In India movie stars who played divine beings in religious epics have turned themselves into politicians. The Ayodhya agitation referred to in Chapter 6 was boosted by television showings of the Ramayana; in

BOX 23

The appropriation of the supernatural—the insistence that it can only be allowed to appear in distinctively Christian forms—is the central theme running through the testimonies that form an important segment in the televangelist Pat Robertson's *700 Club* programmes. Many of these divine interventions involve healings, either from moral sicknesses such as alcoholism or drug abuse, or from physical illnesses such as back pains or arthritis. In one of these programmes a woman suffering from severe pain in her lower back actually claimed to have been healed while watching the *700 Club*. In the television re-enactment viewers see her lying on her couch, while Robertson appears on screen, talking about the Pool of Bethesda where Jesus healed a man who had been crippled for thirty-eight years. While Robertson goes on to pray for healing, the film cuts to the woman in pain on her couch. Then Sheila Walsh, Robertson's female co-anchor appears on the screen and announces: 'The Lord is healing someone with a terrible back. He's put His hand upon you and restored you completely.' The woman then announces: 'I got off the couch and the pain was gone.' A family practitioner confirms that her condition was serious; a chiropracter then exhibits X-rays taken before and after the event, which demonstrate to his apparent satisfaction that a miracle has occurred. The final shot in the film shows the now healthy woman catching her 5-year-old daughter off a playground slide. The studio audience claps and cheers. The segment is followed by studio badinage between Robertson and Walsh:

Robertson (chuckling approvingly): 'Healing is basically when a condition or a disease stops. But re-creation of a joint or ligament, in this case a disc, it is marvellous!'

Walsh (patting her hair): 'It's like I needed a creative miracle on my hair' (Audience laughter).

(Malise Ruthven, reporting a *700 Club*, videotape, 21 July 1992)

the communal rioting that followed, Hindu and Muslim agitators stirred up mutual hostility by showing videos of their co-religionists under attack. (In Brazil, actors, carrying drama into real life, have been known to kill each other offstage.) But over-exposure on television can lead God's spokespersons to become parodies of themselves. In America, where television preachers are well into the second generation, Christian broadcasting is also Christian 'camp'.

In the *700 Club* the supernatural is not just appropriated: it is routinized and domesticated, formatted into a regular 15–20-minute slots. In normal parlance a supernatural event is by definition unpredictable and awe-inspiring, since natural laws have been suspended or superseded. Yet on the *700 Club* healings and other supernatural interventions, in which the divine is presumed to have acted on matter by the invocation of the Holy Spirit through prayer, occur so frequently as to be almost banal. To the outsider Walsh's remark about the need for a miracle on her hair (see box 22) seems an outrageous put-down—both of the healed woman's pain, and of her divinely arranged release from it. But the studio audience—and, one suspects, the average *700 Club* viewer—take it quite differently. For those born-again Christians miracles are routine occurrences—something to make in-group jokes about. In the community of the saved, as exhibited on CBN, God routinely suspends natural laws and processes. The miraculous is thus not so much a manifestation of the inexplicable Power of the Almighty, as the ritual confirmation of a belief-system that challenges the conventions of secular medical science. Like the Bible itself, the miraculous acts as a shibboleth or totem, reinforcing the identity of the group.

Everywhere religious programming is becoming more self-conscious as religious leaders try to get their messages across to increasingly sophisticated audiences. A study of Syrian broadcasts during the holy month of Ramadan in 1995 and 1996 shows that like Christmas in Western countries, Ramadan is a time when families get together and watch a considerable amount of television, much of it entertainment. The religious broadcasts, according to the scholar Andreas Christmann, subtly interweave Ramadan hymns and prayers with images that would seem 'to contradict the rather sparse and iconoclastic visual language of orthodox Islam', with the traditional repertoire of hymns and prayers accompanied by images of prayer halls, minarets, calligraphies, meditating Muslims, and 'romanticised pictures of the Syrian landscape as well as pages from the Quran, slotted in as graphic cards'. The overall effect presents Islam as a national religion, rather as the BBC's *Songs of Praise*—where professionally sung hymns are accompanied by shots that pay homage to the beauties of Britain's landscape and its magnificent cathedrals—celebrates the glories of Britain's national Church (with space, of course, given to non-Anglican communions). After a thorough viewing of two seasons'

Ramadan programmes it became clear to Christmann that they 'attempt to reinforce the notion of belonging to one nation regardless of denomination, ethnicity, class and gender. With strong appeal to the unification of the national community, the main appeal of the televisual message is to harmonize divergent interests and orientations.' In contrast to Robertson, who seeks to restore the God who intervenes supernaturally by means of the airwaves, Syrian television seeks to integrate popular religiosity with the modernist reformism of the Salafi tradition, with the media canalizing 'popular spirituality away from mystical pantheism into more monotheistic spiritual forms'. The invocations played during the popular Iftar programmes transmitted during the fast-breaking meal at sundown contain no references to the guardian spirits or to the efficacy of amulets and talismans, or to visits to the tombs of local saints or leaders of mystical orders. '[B]y conceiving God as non-manipulative and more abstract, television has brought popular religion into closer conformity with Islam's official monotheistic ideals.' Sufi dances, when shown, are rather stiff and low-key. Nothing is shown on television that is suggestive of 'excess, exaggeration or trance'.9

The increase in religious militancy, occurring in many traditions in defiance of the secularization thesis, may be related to the increasing power and accessibility of audiovisual media, but the long-term consequences are ambiguous. In the first instance the fundamentalist impulse in many traditions has been a reaction to the invasive quality of film and television, which exposes 'sacred areas' like sexual relations to public gaze, transgressive images bringing them into the home. During the Islamist campaign in Algeria technicians had their throats slit for fitting satellite dishes that would bring into Muslim homes images of the 'satanic West', including semi-pornographic material from Italy and the Netherlands as well as factual news channels. In America 'televangelists' such as Falwell and Robertson 'fought back' against the perceived secularization of the culture by creating their own religious programmes and television networks. With the development of satellite networks such as the al-Jazeera channel based in Qatar, state-funded broadcasting monopolies are losing their ability to impose censorship and control information. In the least-developed regions even more radical forces for change are at work, as the audio-visual revolution undercuts the authority of the literate elites. Societies such as Iran and India where levels of literacy have been low have moved from the oral to the audio-visual era without experiencing the revolution in literacy that generated both Protestantism and the Enlightenment in Europe.

Clearly the revolution in communications has a bearing on the failure of the secularization thesis as promulgated by Berger, Cox, and others. Where levels of literacy are low the audio and video cassette have enabled charismatic religious figures such as Sheikh Kishk in Egypt and the late Ayatollah Khomeini to acquire massive followings. Osama bin Laden's carefully crafted videos disseminated by al-Jazeera have contributed to his image as the archetypical Islamic hero. Audio-visual technologies restore the power of word and gesture—traditional province of religion—to a new type of leader, undercutting the hegemony of bureaucrats and the traditional religious professionals whose source of information and power was the written word. When relayed on tape or television, the power of orality and the languages of ritual and gesture retain their potency. 'Insult'—perceived through claims made on television rather than in *The Satanic Verses*—triggered the anti-Rushdie agitation in Britain and South Asia. The Ayodhya dispute, which had festered in the courts for decades, only became a national issue in India when everyone could see what was happening. With television the processes whereby village- or family-based identities break down are accelerated, leaving an emotional vacuum to be filled by iconic, charismatic figures such as Bin Laden. Literacy has ceased to be the prerequisite for entering the political realm as it was in the past.

Fundamentalisms have benefited from the revolution in communications in two ways. First, radio broadcasts and television images, which are now accessible to the majority of people on this planet, make people much more aware of issues with which they can identify than was the case in the past. They increase the political temperature and add to perceptions of cultural conflict. An obvious example is the Israeli-Palestinian conflict, with viewers throughout the Muslim world enraged by the sight of Israeli soldiers killing and humiliating Palestinians, while viewers in the West, shocked and dismayed by the carnage inflicted by suicide bombers, are liable to have anti-Arab or anti-Muslim prejudices confirmed. As numerous media theorists have pointed out, television is not the same as propaganda. It does not have a unidirectional or homogenizing impact on viewers. Most viewers bring pre-existing knowledge to what they see and hear on television, 'decoding images' according to their prejudices. In the Muslim world images of Israeli oppression may be reinforced by perceived differences in lifestyles. For example the explicit sexual interactions to be seen on Tel Aviv beach may add to Islamist perceptions that Palestinians are facing not just a 'racist' enemy that discriminates against them, but one that is wholly evil because of its 'pagan' (jahili) social attitudes. Secondly, as explained already, fundamentalists benefit from the 'para-personal', electronically amplified relationships between charismatic leaders and their audiences. Nasser and Hitler were both beneficiaries of the new medium of radio; both Khomeini and Bin Laden were iconically impressive figures able to convey the solemnity, gravitas, nobility, and asceticism Muslims associate with the aniconic image of the Prophet Muhammad.

But if fundamentalist movements benefit from the media revolution, they are also liable to be among its casualties. The development of satellite television and increasing access to the Internet is bringing an end to the information monopolies on which fundamentalists—like other authoritarian movements—depend. In certain contexts, such as Israel-Palestine and Iraq after the Anglo-American invasion, armed resistance to an externally imposed authority, publicized by the media, is regarded as legitimate by a significant number of people. Under such circumstances (which usually fit the category of religious nationalism, rather than 'pure' fundamentalism) the terrorists or martyrs may become heroes. But where religious radicals have tried to impose their will by violence, as in Egypt, the publicity they court by indulging in the 'propaganda of the deed' may result in popular revulsion, especially in the pious middle-class constituencies on which they depend for support. After an exhaustive analysis of modern Islamist movements from Morocco to Indonesia the French political analyst Gilles Kepel has concluded that terrorism is really a sign of failure, deployed when political mobilization has failed. The recurrent violence of the 1990s—the attacks on tourists in Egypt, the Taliban takeover in Afghanistan, the war in Chechnya, the violence in France, the attacks on US targets in Saudi Arabia, Yemen, and East Africa culminating in '9/11' is 'above all a reflection of the movement's structural weakness, not its growing strength'.[10] The decline in the movement's capacity for political mobilization explains why 'such spectacular and devastating new forms of terrorism' were visited on America itself.[11]

Kepel's book was published before Islamist parties took power in Pakistan's North-West Frontier Province following elections imposed by Washington on the Musharraf government. Rumours of the death of Islamism in this area are certainly premature. On a broader canvas, Kepel's analysis may still hold good, but there are frightening dangers along the way. Where Islamists have succeeded in taking power, as in Iran, satellite technology tells against them, since it becomes impossible for them to sustain their monopoly over the religious discourse. Religious texts such as the Koran have endured because they transcend ideologies, speaking to the human condition in language that is always open to alternative interpretations. At the time of writing Iranian opposition forces, with explicit verbal support from the American president, are demonstrating against the clerical leadership whom they accuse of blocking the reformist agenda of President Khatami and the parliament. The demonstrators have been sustained by satellite channels run by Iranian exiles in the United States. Mindful of the fate of the Baathist regime in Iraq and the Taliban in Afghanistan, the Iranian regime appears to be succumbing to international pressure, backed by the United States, to open up its nuclear programme to United Nations weapons inspectors. Libya, once a pariah state, has announced that it is abandoning weapons of mass destruction, a policy aimed at the lifting of United Nations sanctions.

The future is nonetheless precarious. Soon two Islamist

regimes, Iran and Pakistan, could be armed with nuclear weapons, a prospect made more dangerous by the strand of apocalyptic fantasy that excites and inspires the children of Abraham. In Israel-Palestine Jewish fundamentalists, backed by the Israeli army and with support from the Falwellites and other Protestant extremists in America resist US pressure to relinquish control of occupied Palestine, in ironic collusion with the Islamist militants of Hamas and Islamic Jihad. Within three years, at this writing, an Iranian regime with nuclear capacity could be supporting the Palestinians in the next round of the *intifada* against Israel. Since the latter already has its nuclear weapons, the stage will be set for the Armageddon predicted and welcomed by premilliennialists as the necessary prelude to the return of Christ. The gloomy prognosis might be applied, *a fortiori*, to Pakistan, an economic and social disaster zone when compared with its rival, the 'polytheist' or 'pagan' India. More ominously even than in Israel-Palestine, the apocalyptic mood in Pakistan centres on the 'Islamic bomb', to which there are now flower-decked shrines in major cities. Like the attacks on New York and Washington, which like other cities in the Satanic West face the prospect of terrorist attacks with 'dirty bombs' (conventional explosives containing radioactive materials capable of spreading radiation over a large area), Pakistani bomb-worship may be a manifestation of nihilistic theological despair. 'Polytheist' India flourishes compared with rightly-guided Pakistan. So do infidel

places by adding 'scientific creationism' to the curriculum. They inconvenience some women—especially poor women with limited access to travel—by making abortion illegal in certain states. On a planetary level they are selfish, greedy, and stupid, damaging the environment by the excessive use of energy and lobbying against environmental controls. What is the point of saving the planet, they argue, if Jesus is arriving tomorrow?

American fundamentalists are a headache, a thorn in flesh of the *bien-pensant* liberals, the subject of bemused concern to 'Old Europeans' who have experienced too many real catastrophes to yearn for Armageddon. Given that premillennialism and its associated theologies are significant components of American policy, especially under Republican administrations, it seems fair to state that Protestant fundamentalism is a dangerous religion. Whatever spiritual benefits individuals may have gained by taking Jesus as their 'personal saviour' the apocalyptic fantasies harboured by born-again Christians have a negative impact on public policy. Because of its impact on the environment and its baleful role in the Middle East, America's religiosity is a problem.

But the solution is also American. The constitutional separation of church and state is as fundamental to American democracy as the Bible is to fundamentalists. The hard line preached by televangelists such as Falwell and Robertson is protected by the First Amendment, but it is also limited by it. Though fundamentalists can influence policy, they cannot control it. The same considerations apply, by and large, to fundamentalists in Israel, Sri Lanka, and India, who are constrained by the pluralistic and democratic political systems in which they operate.

The Islamic situation is different, because for historical and sociological reasons too complex to explain in this book, very few Muslim political cultures have developed along democratic lines. In their ruthless drive to power, Islamists have succeeded in taking control of the state temporarily in Sudan, Pakistan, and Afghanistan and permanently in Saudi Arabia and (under different sectarian colours) in Iran. Where the Islamist tide has receded or been checked (as in Pakistan, Egypt, and Algeria) it has been ruthless action by the military rather than the constraints of democratic institutions that have protected secular government. The association of religious pluralism and secularism with militarism (as in Syria, Pakistan, and Turkey) rather than with democracy has been an important element in the Islamist rhetorical armory.

Where the military governs along secular lines, as in Algeria or in Turkey during periods of army intervention, Islamists can plausibly appeal to democratic feelings. But where Islamists actually hold power, as in Iran, they resist democratic change as being contrary to the will of God. There are ways out of this vicious spiral, but they require fine political tuning. One example is offered by Turkey, where in order to win democratically Islamists have had to abandon their more strident demands for 're-Islamizing' society. Another is offered by Jordan, which allows Islamists to win parliamentary seats, exposing them to the cut and thrust of political debate.

Despite these very real problems, the call for freedom, even when polluted by the suspicion that it is being exploited by commercial interests, still runs with the grain of popular aspirations. Islamism, like other fundamentalisms, works best in opposition. In power it proves no less susceptible to corruption or manipulation than the ideologies and systems it seeks to supplant. For the foreseeable future Muslim nationalists will doubtless continue to resist American global hegemony, along with Russian imperialism in Transcaucasia and the Israeli subjugation of Palestine. But in other respects the power of modern technology may be working in America's direction. In the age of satellite broadcasting and the internet, pluralism and diversity of choice are no longer aspirations. They are dynamic realities.

NOTES

CHAPTER 1: Family Resemblances

1. Karen McCarthy Brown, 'Fundamentalism and the Control of Women', in John Stratton, *Fundamentalism and Gender* (Oxford: Oxford University Press, 1994), Hawley (ed.), 198.

2. Bruce B. Lawrence, *Defenders of God* (San Francisco: Harper and Row, 1989), 96.

3. Anthony Kenny (ed.), *The Wittgenstein Reader* (Oxford: Blackwell, 1994), 48–9.

4. Paul Boyer, *When Time Shall Be No More: Prophesy Belief in Modern American Culture* (Cambridge, Mass.: Harvard Belknap Press, 1992), 49.

5. Martin E. Marty, 'The Fundamentals of Fundamentalism', in Lawrence Kaplan (ed.), *Fundamentalism in Comparative Perspective* (Amherst, Mass.: University of Massachusetts Press, 1992), 18.

6. Martin E. Marty and R. Scott Appleby, *Accounting for Fundamentalisms* (The Fundamentalism Project, vol. iv: Chicago: Chicago University Press, 1995), 176.

7. Martin E. Marty and R. Scott Appleby, *The Glory and the Power* (Boston: Beacon Press, 1992), 120.

8. Garry Wills, *Under God: Religion and American Politics* (New York: Simon and Schuster, 1990), 98.

9. Ibid. 108.

10. Adolf Hitler, speech 22 Aug. 1939, cited in Ernst Nolte, *Three Faces of Fascism* (New York: Mentor, 1969), 443; Mark Neocleous, *Fascism* (Buckingham: Open University Press, 1997), 16.

11. Susan F. Harding, *The Book of Jerry Falwell* (Princeton: Princeton University Press, 2000), 75.

12. Ibid. 75–6.

13. Steve Bruce, *The Rise and Fall of the New Christian Right* (Oxford: Oxford University Press, 1988), 171.

14. E. C. Hodgkin (ed.), *Two Kings in Arabia—Sir Reader Bullard's Letters from Jeddah* (Reading: Ithaca Press, 1993), 167–8.

15. Lawrence, *Defenders of God*, 272 n. 10.

16. Jane Kelsey, *Economic Fundamentalism* (London: Pluto Press, 2000), 2.

17. For accounts of the 'Fundies' among the German Greens and the issues dividing the movement, see Ian Traynor, *Guardian*, 5 July 1999; Gary Younge, *Guardian*, 6 July 2000; Dennis Staunton, *Observer*, 25 June 2000.

CHAPTER 2: The Scandal of Difference

1. Sayyid Qutb. *Fi Zilal al-Quran* (Beimt: Dar al-Shuruq 1981) vol. I 510–11 cited by Youssef M. Choueiri *Islamic Fundamentalism* (Boston Twayne, 1990), 124.

2. Ibid.

3. Steve Bruce, 'Revelations: The Future of the New Christian Right', in Lawrence Kaplan (ed.), *Fundamentalism in Comparative Perspective* (Amherst, Mass.: University of Massachusetts Press, 1992), 58.

4. CBS (New York), 3 Oct. 2002; www.escapefromwatchtower.com/falwell.html

5. Martin E. Marty, 'The Fundamentals of Fundamentalism', in Lawrence Kaplan (ed.), *Fundamentalism in Comparative Perspective* (Amherst, Mass.: University of Massachusetts Press, 1992), 18.

6. Bruce, 'Revelations', 60.

7. Quoted in Ernst Cassirer, *The Philosophy of the Enlightenment*, trans. Fritz C. Aa Koelln and James P. Pettegrove (Princeton: Princeton University Press, 1951), 175.

8. Will Herberg, *Protestant, Catholic, Jew, an Essay in American Religious Sociology* (New York Anchor Books, 1960), 86.

9. Bruce, 'Revelations', 43.

CHAPTER 3: The Snares of Literalism

1. Nancy Tatom Ammerman, *Bible Believers: Fundamentalists in the Modern World* (New Brunswick: Rutgers University Press, 1987), 6.

2. George Dollar, *History of Fundamentalism in America*, quoted in Lawrence, *Defenders of God*, 161.

3. James Barr, *Fundamentalism* (Philadelphia: Westminster Press, 1978), 41.

4. Vincent Crapanzano, *Serving the Word: Literalism in America from the Pulpit to the Bench* (New York: The New Press, 2000), 14.

5. Ibid. 17.

6. Richard Elliott Friedman, *Who Wrote the Bible?* (New York: Harper and Row, 1987; paperback edn 1989), 28.

7. Barr, *Fundamentalism*, 61.

8. Maurice Bucaille, *The Bible, the Qur'an and Science*, trans. Alastair D. Pannell and the author (Indianapolis: American Trust Publications, 1979).

9. Barr, *Fundamentalism*, 173.

10. Joshua 3: 13–17.

11. Barr, *Fundamentalism*, 236.

12. Barr, *Fundamentalism*, 245.

13. Barr, *Fundamentalism*, 257.

14. Koran 22: 5.

15. John A. Coleman, 'Catholic Integralism as a Fundamentalism', in Lawrence Kaplan (ed.), *Fundamentalism in Comparative Perspective* (Amherst, Mass.: University of Massachusetts Press, 1992), 7.

16. Daniel Alexander, 'Is Fundamentalism an Integrism?', *Social Compass*, 32/4 (1985), 380; cited in Coleman, 'Catholic Integralism', 87.

17. Alexander, 'Is Fundamentalism an Integrism', 379–80; Coleman, 85.

18. Ibid. 87.

19. Ibid.

20. Steve Brower, Paul Gifford, and Susan D. Rose, *Exporting the American Gospel* (New York and London: Routledge, 1998), 57.

21. Coleman, 'Catholic Integralism', 84.

22. Ibid. 85.

23. Ibid. 86.

24. Barr, *Fundamentalism*, 57.

25. R. Bell and W. M. Watt, *Introduction to the Quran* (Edinburgh: Edinburgh University Press, 1977), 66.

26. John Wansbrough, *Quranic Studies: Sources and Methods of Scriptural Interpretation* (Oxford: Oxford University Press, 1977); *The Sectarian Milieu: Content and Composition of Islamic Salvation History* (Oxford: Oxford University Press, 1978).

27. G. R. Hawting, *The Idea of Idolatry and the Emergence of Islam: from Polemic to History* (Cambridge: Cambridge University Press, 1999), 7.

28. Karen Armstrong, *The Battle for God—Fundamentalism in Judaism, Christianity and Islam* (London: HarperCollins, 2000), p. xiii.

29. Ibid. 337.

30. Anthony Giddens, *The Consequences of Modernity* (Stanford, Calif.: Stanford University Press, 1990), 112–13.

31. Ibid. 121 ff.

32. Ibid. 34–6, 124 ff.

33. Pascal Boyer, *Religion Explained: The Human Instincts that Fashion Gods, Spirits and Ancestors* (London: Vintage, 2002), 116.

34. Niels C. Nielson, Jr, *Fundamentalism, Mythos and World Religions* (Albany, NY: SUNY Press, 1993), 59.

35. Kathleen Raine, *Blake and the New Age* (London: Allen and Unwin, 1979).

36. Malise Ruthven, *The Divine Supermarket: Shopping for God in America* (New York: Morrow, 1990), 236.

37. Adapted from Sayyid Qutb, *Milestones: A Translation of Ma'alim fi-l tariq* (New Delhi: Markazi Maktaba Islami, 1981), 27.

38. Deuteronomy 25:17–19 (Contemporary English version).

39. *Bat Kol*, 26 Feb. 1980, cited by Yehoshafat Harkabi, *Israel's Fateful Decisions* (London: I. B. Tauris, 1988), 153.

40. Ian Lustick, *For the Land and the Lord: Jewish Fundamentalism in Israel* (New York: Council on Foreign Relations, 1988), 68–9.

41. Cited by James Thrower, *Marxist-Leninist 'Scientific Atheism' and the Study of Religion in the USSR* (The Hague: Mouton, 1983), 369.

CHAPTER 4: Controlling Women

1. All the details of Roop Kanwar's *sati* and the ensuing controversy in this chapter are taken from John Stratton Hawley, 'Hinduism: Sati and its Defenders', in John Stratton Hawley (ed.), *Fundamentalism and Gender* (New York: Oxford University Press, 1994), 79 ff. and Sakuntala Narasimhan, *Sati: A Study of Widow Burning in India* (New Delhi: HarperCollins, 1998).

2. Ibid. 41.

3. Ibid. 183; Hawley, 'Hinduism', 96.

4. Ibid.

5. Ibid. 90.

6. Martin Riesebrodt, *Pious Passion—The Emergence of Modern Fundamentalism in the United States and Iran*, trans. Don Renau (Berkeley: University of California Press, 1993).

7. Riesebrodt, *Pious Passion*, 128.

8. Ibid. 176–7.

9. Helen Hardacre, 'The Impact of Fundamentalisms on Women, the Family and Interpersonal Relations', in Martin E. Marty and R. Scott Appleby (eds), *Fundamentalism and Society* (Chicago: University of Chicago Press, 1993), 129.

10. Ibid. 130.

11. Jorge E. Maldonado, 'Building "Fundamentalism" from the Family in Latin America', in Marty and Appleby, *Fundamentalism and Society*, 235.

12. Andrea B. Rugh, 'Reshaping Personal Relations in Egypt', in Marty and Appleby, *Fundamentalism and Society*, 151–80.

13. Valentine M. Moghadam, 'Fundamentalism and the Woman Question in Afghanistan', in Lawrence Kaplan (ed.), *Fundamentalism in Comparative Perspective* (Amherst, Mass.: University of Massachusetts Press, 1992), 134.

14. Ibid. 135.

15. Ibid. 137.
16. Hawley, *Fundamentalism and Gender*, 26.
17. Judy Brink and Joan Mencher (eds), *Mixed Blessings: Gender and Religious Fundamentalisms Cross Culturally* (London/New York: Routledge, 1997), 3.
18. Cited in Hawley, *Fundamentalism and Gender*, 100.
19. See Jean Holm (ed.) with John Bowker, *Women in Religion* (London: Pinter, 1994), 36.
20. Hardacre, 'The Impact of Fundamentalisms', 143.
21. Ibid. 142.
22. Ibid. 141.
23. Ibid. 145.
24. Steve Bruce, *Rise and Fall of the New Christian Right* (Oxford: Oxford University Press, 1988), 142.
25. Giles Fraser, 'Evangelicals have become this century's witch-burners', *Guardian*, 14 July 2003.
26. Brenda Brasher, *Godly Women: Fundamentalism and Female* Power (New Brunswick, NJ: Rutgers University Press, 1998), 121.
27. Ibid. 173.
28. Ibid. 172.
29. Ibid.
30. Ibid. 168.
31. Frances Fitzgerald, *Cities on a Hill* (New York: Simon and Schuster, 1986), p. 141; Brasher, *Godly Women*, 169.
32. Anita Weiss, in Akbar S. Ahmed and Hastings Donnan (eds), *Islam, Globalization and Postmodernity* (London: Routledge, 1994), 137.
33. Michael Gilsenan, *Lords of the Lebanese Marches: Violence and Narrative in an Arab Society* (London: I. B. Tauris, 1996), 189.

CHAPTER 5: Fundamentalism and Nationalism I

1. Steve Brower, Paul Gifford, and Susan D. Rose, *Exporting the American Gospel* (New York and London: Routledge, 1998), 15.
2. Ibid.

3. Ibid. 345.

4. Pat Robertson, *The Turning Tide: The Fall of Liberalism and the Rise of Common Sense* (Dallas World Publishing, 1993), 294–7.

5. Bruce B. Lawrence, *Defenders of God—The Fundamentalist Revolt against the Modern Age* (San Francisco: Harper and Row, 1989), 83.

6. Charles Adams in John Esposito (ed.), *Voices of Resurgent Islam* (New York: Oxford University Press, 1983), 103.

7. Rafiuddin Ahmed 'Redefining Muslim Identity in South Asia' in Martin E. Marty and R. Scott Appleby (eds), *Accounting for Fundamentalisms* (The Fundamentalism Project vol. iv: Chicago: University of Chicago Press, 1996), 675.

8. Ibid.

9. Lawrence, *Defenders of God*, 200.

10. John Hutchinson and Anthony D. Smith (eds), *Nationalism* (Oxford: Oxford University Press, 1994), 7.

11. Albert Hourani, *A History of the Arab Peoples* (London: Faber; rev. edn 2002), 138.

12. Paul Berman, 'The Philosopher of Islamic Terror', *New York Times Magazine*, 23 Mar. 2003. I am grateful to David Hayes of *Open Democracy* for sending me this article.

13. Mark Juergensmeyer, *The New Cold War? Religious Nationalism Confronts the Secular State* (Berkeley: University of California Press, 1993), 15.

14. Ahmed Rouadjia, 'Discourse and Strategy of the Algerian Islamist Movement (1986–1992)', in Laura Guazzone (ed.), *The Islamist Dilemma: The Political Role of Islamist Movements in the Contemporary Arab World* (Reading: Ithaca Press, 1995), 75.

15. Ibid. 99.

16. Ibid. 10. Cf. Olivier Roy, *The Failure of Political Islam* (London: I. B. Tauris, 1994).

17. Guazzone, *The Islamist Dilemma*, 11.

18. *Sudan Democratic Gazette*, 34 (Mar. 1993), cited by Hayder Ibrahim Alki, 'Islamism in Practice: The Case of Sudan', in Guazzone, *The Islamist Dilemma*, 207.

19. Gilles Kepel, *Jihad: The Trail of Political Islam* (London: I. B. Tauris, 2002), 183.

CHAPTER 6: Fundamentalism and Nationalism II

1. Anthony D. Smith, *Chosen Peoples: Sacred Foundations of National Identity* (Oxford: Oxford Unversity Press, 2004).

2. Text in Dorothy Macardle, *The Irish Republic* (London: Corgi, rev. edn 1968), 127–8.

3. Sybil Sheridan, 'Judaism', in Jean Holm and John Bowker (eds), *Myth and History* (London: Pinter, 1994), 120.

4. Ibid.

5. Rudolf Bultmann, *History and Eschatology* (Edinburgh: Edinburgh University Press, 1957), 120–1.

6. Ian Lustick, *For the Land and the Lord: Jewish Fundamentalism in Israel* (New York: Council on Foreign Relations, 1988), 99.

7. *Year by Year* 5728, ed. Rabbi Picknik (Jerusalem: 1967), 109.

8. Quoted in *Ha'aretz* by S. Abramov, 30 May 1985.

9. *Nekudah*, 73 (Oct. 1985).

10. Nahum Barnea, *Yediot Aharonot*, 27 Feb. 1994, quoted by Shahak.

11. Yuval Katz in *Yerushalaim* weekly, Jerusalem, 4 Mar. 1994.

12. Michael Karpin and Ina Friedman, *Murder in the Name of God: The Plot to Kill Yitzhak Rabin* (London: Granta, 1999), 120.

13. A translation of al-Farraj's famous tract *al-farida al-ghaiba* (variously translated as 'The Hidden Imperative', 'The Missing Precept', or 'The Neglected Duty') and the official *ulama* riposte is discussed at length in Johannes J. G. Jansen, *The Neglected Duty: The Creed of Sadat's Assassins and Islamic Resurgence in the Middle East* (New York: Macmillan, 1986); see also Gilles Kepel, *The Prophet and Pharaoh: Muslim Extremism in Egypt*, trans. Jon Rothschild (London: Saqi Books, 1985).

14. Karpin and Friedman, *Murder in the Name of God*, 130.

15. Quoted in Smith, *Chosen Peoples*.

16. Mark Juergensmeyer, *Terror in the Mind of God: The Global Rise of Religious Violence* (Berkeley: University of California Press, 2000), 153.

17. Jehoshafat Harkabi, *Israel's Fateful Decisions* (London: I. B. Tauris, 1988), 153.

18. Steve Bruce, *Fundamentalism* (Cambridge: Polity Press, 2000), 97.

19. Ibid. 96.

20. Daniel Gold, 'Organised Hinduisms', in Martin E. Marty and R. Scott Appleby (eds), *Fundamentalisms Observed* (Chicago: University of Chicago Press, 1991), 542.

21. Ibid. 537.

22. Ibid. 545.

23. See Malise Ruthven, *A Fury for God: The Islamist Attack on America* (London: Granta, 2002), 89.

24. Gold, 'Organized Hinduisms', 539.

25. Juergensmeyer, *Terror in the Mind of God*, 78.

26. Gold, 'Organized Hinduisms', 563.

27. Ibid. 547.

28. Ibid. 549.

29. Ibid. 566.

30. Ibid. 580.

31. Sunil Khilnani, *The Idea of India* (London: Hamish Hamilton, 1997), 33.

32. Ibid. 34.

33. Gold, 'Organized Hinduisms', 280.

34. T. N. Madan, 'The Double-edged Sword: Fundamentalism and the Sikh Religious Tradition', in Marty and Appleby, *Fundamentalisms Observed*, 594.

35. Ibid. 603.

36. Ibid. 620.

37. *International Herald Tribune*, 27 May 2003, p. 5.

38. Personal testimonies given to me by Muslim residents of Bombay, April 1996.

39. Donald K. Swearer, 'Fundamentalist Movements in Theravada Buddhism', in Marty and Appleby, *Fundamentalisms Observed*, 633.

40. Ibid. 638.

41. Ibid. 640.

42. Ibid. 650.

43. S. N. Eisenstadt, *Fundamentalism, Sectarianism and Revolution* (Cambridge: Cambridge University Press, 2000), 91.

44. Ibid. 206.
45. Juergensmeyer, *Terror in the Mind of God*, 156.
46. Ibid.
47. Ibid. 161.
48. Ibid.
49. Ibid. 159.

CHAPTER 7: Conclusion

1. 'Religion in Post-Protestant America', *Commentary*, May 1986.
2. Ibid.
3. Jeff Haynes, 'Religion, Secularisation and Politics: A Postmodern Conspectus', *Third World Quarterly*, 18/ [vol. 18, no. 4] (1997), 715.
4. Ibid. 716, citing M. Watson 'Christianity and the Green Option in the New Europe', in J. Fulton and P. Gee (eds), *Religion in Contemporary Europe* (Lewiston, NY: Edwin Mellen, 1994), 150.
5. *International Herald Tribune*, 16 June 2003.
6. Anson Shupe and Jeffrey K. Hadden, 'Is there such a thing as global fundamentalism?' in Anson Shupe and Jeffrey K. Hadden (eds), *Secularization and Fundamentalism Reconsidered* (New York: Paragon House, 1989), 112.
7. Ibid.
8. Steve Bruce, *The Rise and Fall of the New Christian Right* (Oxford: Clarendon Press, 1988), 127.
9. Andreas Christmann, 'An Invented Piety: Ramadan on Syrian TV', Paper presented at a conference on Religion and the Media organized by the British Association for the Study of Religion, Lancaster, November 1996. I am thankful to Dr. Christmann for sending me a copy of his paper.
10. Gilles Kepel, *Jihad: The Trail of Political Islam* (London: I. B. Tauris, 2002), 207.
11. Ibid. 4.
12. Malise Ruthven, *A Fury for God: The Islamist Attack on America* (London: Granta, 2002), 132–3.

SELECT BIBLIOGRAPHY

al-Afghani, Jamal al-Din, *al-Radd ala al-Dahriyyin*, trans. Nikki Keddie in *An Islamic Response to Imperialism* (Berkeley: University of California Press, 1968).

Ammerman, Nancy Tatom, *Bible Believers—Fundamentalists in the Modern World* (New Brunswick, NJ: Rutgers University Press, 1987).

Armstrong, Karen, *The Battle for God Fundamentalism in Judaism, Christianity and Islam* (London: HarperCollins, 2000).

Barber, Benjamin R., *Jihad vs McWorld: How Globalism and Tribalism are Reshaping the World* (New York: Ballantine Books, 1995).

Barr, James, *Fundamentalism* (Philadelphia: Westminster Press, 1978).

Beinin, Joel, and Stork, Joe (eds), *Political Islam: Essays from Middle East Report* (London: I. B. Tauris, 1997).

Binder, Leonard, *Islamic Liberalism: A Critique of Development Ideologies* (Chicago: Chicago University Press, 1988).

Bloom, Harold, *The American Religion: The Emergence of the Post-Christian Nation* (New York: Simon and Schuster, 1991).

Boyer, Pascal, *Religion Explained: The Human Instincts that Fashion Gods, Spirits and Ancestors* (London: Vintage, 2002).

Boyer, Paul, *When Time Shall Be No More: Prophesy Belief in Modern American Culture* (Cambridge, Mass.: Harvard University Press, 1992).

Brower, Steve, Gifford, Paul, and Rose, Susan D., *Exporting the American Gospel* (New York and London: Routledge, 1998).

Bruce, Steve, *The Rise and Fall of the New Christian Right* (Oxford: Oxford University Press, 1988).

—— *God Save Ulster: The Religion and Politics of Paisleyism* (New York: Oxford University Press, 1989).

—— *Fundamentalism* (Cambridge: Polity Press, 2000).

Bultmann, Rudolf, *History and Eschatology* (Edinburgh: Edinburgh University Press, 1957).

Caplan, Lionel (ed.), *Studies in Religious Fundamentalism* (Albany, NY: SUNY Press, 1987).

Choueiri, Youssef M., *Islamic Fundamentalism* (Boston, Mass.: Twayne, 1990).

Cox, Harvey, *The Secular City: Secularization and Urbanization in Theological Perspective* (New York: Macmillan 1965/1990).

Crapanzano, Vincent, *Serving the Word: Literalism in America from the Pulpit to the Bench* (New York: The New Press, 2000).

Cupitt, Don, *The Sea of Faith* (London: BBC, 1984).

Durant, John (ed.), *Darwinism & Divinity: Essays on Evolution and Religious Belief* (Oxford: Blackwell, 1985).

Eisenstadt, S. N., *Fundamentalism, Sectarianism and Revolution* (Cambridge: Cambridge University Press, 2000).

Esposito, John L. (ed.), *Voices of Resurgent Islam* (New York: Oxford University Press, 1983).

—— *The Islamic Threat—Myth or Reality?* (New York: Oxford University Press, 1994).

—— (ed.), *The Oxford Encyclopedia of the Modern Islamic World*, 4 vols (New York: Oxford University Press, 1996).

Gardell, Mattias, *Countdown to Armageddon: Louis Farrakhan and the Nation of Islam* (London: Hurst, 1996).

Gellner, Ernest, *Postmodernism, Reason and Religion* (London: Routledge, 1992).

Giddens, Anthony, *The Consequences of Modernity* (Stanford, Calif.: Stanford University Press, 1990).

Graham, Billy, *The Holy Spirit: Activating God's Power in Your Life* (London: Collins, 1979).

Harding, Susan F., *The Book of Jerry Falwell: Fundamentalist Language and Politics* (Princeton: Princeton University Press, 2000).

Harrell, Jr, David Edwin, *Oral Roberts— An American Life* (Bloomington, Ind.: Indiana University Press, 1985).

Hawley, John Stratton (ed.), *Fundamentalism and Gender* (Oxford: Oxford University Press, 1994).

Humphreys, Stephen R., *Islamic History, A Framework for Inquiry* (Princeton: Princeton University Press, 1991).

Hunter, James Davison, *American Evangelicalism: Conservative Religion and the Quandry of Modernity* (New Brunswick, NJ: Rutgers University Press, 1983).

Hutchinson, John, and Smith, Anthony D. (eds), *Nationalism* (Oxford: Oxford University Press, 1994).

Ibrahim, Saad al-Din, and Hopkins, Nicholas (eds), *Arab Society: Social Science Perspectives* (Cairo: American University in Cairo Press, 1985) (includes Ibrahim's path-breaking article on Egypt's Islamic militants).

al-Jabarti, Abd al-Rahman, *Napoleon in Egypt: al-Jabarti's Chronicle of the French Occupation 1798*, trans. Shmuel Moreh (Princeton: Markus Weiner, 1997).

Juergensmeyer, Mark, *The New Cold War? Religious Nationalism Confronts the Secular State* (Berkeley and Los Angeles: University of California Press, 1993).

—— *Terror in the Mind of God: The Global Rise of Religious Violence* (Berkeley and Los Angeles: University of California Press, 2001).

Kaplan, Lawrence (ed.), *Fundamentalism in Comparative Perspective* (Amherst, Mass.: University of Massachusetts Press, 1992).

Kenny, Anthony (ed.), *The Wittgenstein Reader* (Oxford: Blackwell, 1994).

Kepel, Gilles, *The Prophet and Pharaoh: Muslim Extremism in Egypt*, trans. Jon Rothschild (London: Saqi Books, 1985).

—— *The Revenge of God: The Resurgence of Islam, Christianity and Judaism in the Modern World* (Oxford: Polity Press, 1994).

—— *Allah in the West: Islamic Movements in America and Europe*, trans. Susan Milner (Cambridge: Polity Press, 1997).

—— *Jihad: The Trail of Political Islam* (London: I. B. Tauris, 2002).

Kitcher, Philip, *Abusing Science: The Case against Creationism* (Cambridge, Mass.: MIT Press, 1982).

Lambton, A. K. S., *Islamic Fundamentalism* (London: Royal Asiatic Society, 1989).

Landau, David, *Piety and Power: The World of Jewish Fundamentalism* (London: Secker and Warburg, 1994).

Lawrence, Bruce B., *Defenders of God: The Fundamentalist Revolt against the Modern Age* (San Francisco: Harper and Row, 1989).

Lewis, Philip, *Islamic Britain: Religion, Politics and Identity among British Muslims* (London: I. B. Tauris, 1996).

Lustick, Ian, *For the Land and the Lord: Jewish Fundamentalism in Israel* (New York: Council on Foreign Relations, 1988).

McLuhan, Marshall, *The Gutenberg Galaxy: The Making of Typographic Man* (London: Routledge and Kegan Paul, 1962).

Marsden, George M., *Fundamentalism in American Culture* (New York: Oxford University Press, 1980).

—— *Understanding Fundamentalism and Evangelicalism* (Grand Rapids, Mich.: Eerdmans, 1991).

Martin, William, *The Billy Graham Story: A Prophet with Honour* (London: Hutchinson, 1992).

Marty, Martin E., and Appleby, R. Scott (eds), The Fundamentalism
  Project (Chicago: Chicago University Press, 1991–5), vol. i:
  Fundamentalisms Observed; vol. ii: *Fundamentalisms and Society:
  Reclaiming the Religious Sciences, the Family and Education*; vol. iii:
  *Fundamentalisms and the State: Remaking Polities, Economies and
  Militance*; vol. iv: *Accounting for Fundamentalisms: The Dynamic
  Character of Movements*; vol. v: *Fundamentalisms Comprehended*.

Marty, Martin E., and Appleby, R. Scott, *The Glory and the Power: The
  Fundamentalist Challenge to the Modern World* (Boston, Mass.:
  Beacon Press, 1992).

Mawdudi, Sayyid Abu Ala, *The Religion of Truth* (Lahore: Islamic
  Publications 1967).

Morris, Henry, *The Remarkable Birth of Planet Earth* (San Diego:
  Institute of Creation Science, 1986).

Narasimhan, Sakuntala, *Sati: A Study of Widow Burning in India* (New
  Delhi: HarperCollins, 1998).

Nielsen Jr, Niels C., *Fundamentalism, Mythos and World Religions*
  (Albany, NY: SUNY Press, 1993).

Packer, J. I., *'Fundamentalism' and the Word of God* (Grand Rapids,
  Mich.: Eerdmans, 1958).

Qutb, Sayyid, *Milestones on the Road: A Translation of Maalim fi'l tariq*
  (New Delhi: Markazi Maktaba Islami, 1981, 2000).

Rashid, Ahmed, *Taliban: Islam, Oil and the New Great Game in Central
  Asia* (London: I. B. Tauris, 2002).

Riesebrodt, Martin, *Pious Passion: The Emergence of Modern
  Fundamentalism in the United States and Iran* (Berkeley: University
  of California Press, 1993).

Robertson, Pat, *The Turning Tide: The Fall of Liberalism and the Rise of
  Common Sense* (Dallas: World Publishing, 1993).

Roy, Olivier, *The Failure of Political Islam*, trans. Carol Volk (London:
  I. B. Tauris, 1996).

Ruthven, Malise, *The Divine Supermarket: Shopping for God in America* (New York: Morrow, 1990).

—— *A Satanic Affair: Salman Rushdie and the Wrath of Islam* (London: Hogarth, 1990).

—— *Islam in the World* (London: Penguin, 1994/2000).

—— *A Fury for God: The Islamist Attack on America* (London: Granta, 2002).

Schaeffer, Francis A., *A Christian Manifesto* (London: SPCK, 1981).

Simon, Merrill, *Jerry Falwell and the Jews* (Middle Village, NY: Jonathan David, 1984, 1999).

'Warrack, Ibn', *Why I am not a Muslim* (Amherst, Mass.: University of Massachusetts Press, 1995).

INDEX

Index

Index

Index

Index

Index

Index

Index